CASTLES OF THE CRUSADERS

CASTLES OF THE CRUSADERS

WOLFGANG MÜLLER-WIENER

PHOTOGRAPHS BY A. F. KERSTING

McGRAW-HILL BOOK COMPANY · NEW YORK · TORONTO

Translated from the German by J. Maxwell Brownjohn
This edition © 1966 by Thames and Hudson, London
Library of Congress Catalog Card Number 66-24887
43997
Printed in West Germany

CONTENTS

INTRODUCTION 7

   THE EXPEDITION TO THE HOLY LAND 9

   CONQUEST OF THE HOLY LAND 11

   BALANCE OF POWER 15

   HATTIN 19

   THE KINGDOM OF ACRE 22

   THE KINGDOM OF LESSER ARMENIA 29

   THE LATIN EMPIRE OF CONSTANTINOPLE AND THE FRANKISH DOMAINS OF MOREA . 32

   THE KINGDOM OF CYPRUS 34

   HOSPITALLERS IN THE AEGEAN 37

THE CASTLES 41

   NOTES ON THE PLATES 95

   MAP SHOWING THE SITES OF THE CASTLES 108-109

   GENERAL BIBLIOGRAPHY 110

   INDEX OF PRINCIPAL CASTLES 112

   ACKNOWLEDGEMENTS 113

   THE PLATES 115

INTRODUCTION

One of the most fascinating and mysterious periods in the history of medieval Europe dawned when, at the end of the 11th century and for almost four hundred years thereafter, thousands of peasants and princes, burghers and barons felt impelled by a strange combination of naive piety, greed, and daring, to abandon their native lands for the hazards of the Crusades; when valiant knights wore the sign of the Cross over their chain mail and bishops charged Muslim warriors with sword in hand; when a youthful Europe, groping for a continent beyond its borders, first sought to gain a foothold on alien soil. The earliest expedition to Jerusalem demonstrated that those who marched eastwards beneath the banner of the Cross were not thinking solely of the grand design which had been preached to them. Far from it. For all their religious devotion and spirit of self-sacrifice, prince and vassal were quite capable of pursuing selfish interests and material aims. Self-aggrandizement and self-enrichment were equally powerful motives from the outset, and their strength increased in proportion as Outremer – the land where each was free to seek his fortune – became independent of the occidental Powers. Having intensified itself to an almost inconceivable extent, this blind and selfish quest for power and material possessions ultimately destroyed all that had been built up over the centuries by courage and religious faith, stratagem and daring, self-sacrifice and arduous endeavour.

The need to safeguard their possessions against the dispossessed inhabitants of a strange and far-flung land prompted the invaders to occupy and build castles and walled towns which would not only protect them and their chattels but enable them to hold their adversaries in check. Castles and fortified towns did not spring up in the Holy Land alone. For five hundred miles, from the shores of the Red Sea to the banks of the Euphrates, the narrow strip of Frankish-held territory – little more than sixty miles across at its widest point – was guarded by a chain of interdependent Frankish fortresses. Castles belonging to knights who fought beneath the sign of the Cross were scattered widely over the coasts and islands of the Eastern Mediterranean. Frankish fortresses sprang up on the rocky heights of Cyprus, on the Athenian acropolis and the mountains of Greece, and for decades after the West's last feeble thrusts had petered out, knights in heavy armour stood guard against the Turks in the Aegean and on the coasts of Asia Minor. Many of their strongholds represent milestones in the development of Western fortification and are among the finest products of medieval European architecture.

If we wish to acquire a genuine knowledge of the origin and decline of buildings which are so widely separated, both in time and place, it is not enough to study one or other of them out of context and analyse it for potential influences of various kinds. Castles were never built for their own sake but always for a specific purpose, and the history of many of them shows that once they had fulfilled that purpose they were abandoned and allowed to fall into decay. As a building, the castle can only be understood fully in relation to its political and strategic status and the historical circumstances which prevailed while it was being built. Only from these circumstances can the many different constituents which determined the form of the whole be recognized and distinguished from one another. Historical relationships – and, thus, local peculiarities and traditions – played an even more influential, if not decisive, role in the lands conquered by the Crusaders than in Western Europe (an essentially homogeneous area despite its manifold national differences), for they were lands which had for centuries been repositories of great civilizations, and the last vestiges of those civilizations were preserved in their peoples.

The site of each castle was dictated in general by the geographical and strategic requirements of the current political situation and, in particular, by existing settlements and previous fortifications, roads and fords, mountain passes and good anchorages. The style, general lay-out and ground-plan of the buildings which grew up on these sites were not, however, determined solely by geographical and strategic requirements but influenced in equal measure by local architectural traditions instilled during centuries of Roman, Byzantine, Arab or Armenian sovereignty. Owing to our limited knowledge of the art of fortification in general and early medieval fortification in particular, we are still unable to ascertain how far formative development was influenced by the traditions and experience which the new seigneurs brought with them from their native lands. Imported traditions certainly played a significant part, even though they took second place – at least initially – to that element in local traditions which exerted an influence simply because numerous existing fortresses continued to be used in their original state, and because most of the new ones were constructed by locally resident stone-masons and labourers using such materials as were available on the spot. As time progressed, this predominance of local influence in the development of design, techniques of fortification and workmanship waned under the impact of the wide experience acquired by Frankish knights during long years of siege warfare and military expeditions in neighbouring territories. Indeed, as many Frankish buildings of the 12th and 13th centuries clearly show, local tradition seems to have been overshadowed, where individual formative development was concerned, by the importation of stylistic elements from Western Europe.

The buildings under examination are thus compounded of innumerable different ingredients blended in very different proportions. To form any definite conclusions here would necessitate a comprehensive survey of the various cultural zones and their history, an intimate knowledge of numerous countries and their special characteristics, and, above all, years of travel and research at the site of each architectural relic. All that the limited resources of a lone individual can achieve today is a general and often over-simplified review of the current state of knowledge in this specialized field. My choice of the sites which will be examined in greater detail below has generally been dictated by their state of preservation, in some cases –

I regret to say – by current political conditions, and by a belief that Frankish castles should be viewed, not in isolation, but in close conjunction with contemporary fortifications in neighbouring countries; that is to say, with Arab strongholds and Armenian castles. The scope of the present work precludes any widespread references to Byzantine architectural antecedents, desirable as this would often have been. It also permits only isolated allusions to the influence of Frankish fortification on that of Europe, although this was undoubtedly one field in which the Crusades yielded positive results.

THE EXPEDITION TO THE HOLY LAND   1096-1099

At the Council of Clermont in 1095, Pope Urban II summoned Western Christendom to liberate its brothers in the East, and before long thousands had succumbed to the prevailing mood of fanatical fervour. Two minor expeditions undertaken in the first flush of enthusiasm had already ended in sanguinary failure when elements of the first Crusader army, led by Duke Godfrey of Bouillon and Counts Hugh of Vermandois, Raymond of Toulouse and Bohemond of Tarentum, assembled beneath the walls of the imperial city of Constantinople during the winter of 1096-7. When spring came, the Frankish forces crossed the Hellespont accompanied by units of the Byzantine army and marched on Nicaea, which had been occupied by the Turks for some years past. The town was taken after a brief siege. Here, as when marching through the Balkans and bivouacking beneath the walls of Constantinople, the Franks encountered massive Byzantine fortifications which were unequalled by anything in contemporary Europe. They encountered similar fortifications again and again during their continued advance down the old Byzantine military road. Passing Dorylaeum and Poly-botos, Philomelium and Iconium, the Frankish army reached the Cilician Gates.

Here Baldwin of Boulogne and Tancred the Norman left the army. Taking independent routes, they crossed the passes and debouched into the Cilician plain, where they began, with Armenian support, to reduce towns defended by weak Turkish garrisons. The two Frankish commanders soon quarrelled over possession of the captured towns, however, so Baldwin pushed on further and advanced rapidly eastwards. Aided by the Armenians who had been resident in the area between the Taurus Mountains and the Euphrates for some decades, and with whom he had established cordial relations at Nicaea, Baldwin quickly founded a feudal state of his own. This domain, which straddled the upper reaches of the Euphrates, became known as the County of Edessa.

Meanwhile, the main army had advanced in a wide detour, via Caesarea (Kayseri) and Germanicea (Maraş), on the large and heavily fortified city of Antioch. This fortress represented an obstacle to the army's further advance. It could not be by-passed nor left in the rear of the advancing army without endangering its further progress – especially as Bohemond of

Tarentum had obviously been determined from the outset to establish a personal domain in defiance of the oath of allegiance he had sworn to the Emperor of Byzantium. It took the combined strength of the entire army to besiege Antioch. In the spring of 1098, after seven months of blockade and the construction of three small siege-castles, the city fell to the Franks as a result of treachery. Even then, they did not capture the citadel until they had decisively defeated a large Turkish relieving force.

On the way to Antioch, just as on their march through Cilicia and subsequent advance through Syria and Palestine, the Frankish knights were once more confronted by numerous fortresses which had once been Byzantine but were now occupied by the Muslims. The change in political relationships and economic conditions that had come about since the Arab conquest in the middle of the 7th century had produced many radical alterations in the population density of these erstwhile Byzantine areas. Many a once thriving settlement had been completely abandoned and many towns had dwindled to the size of villages, though the latter still retained their fortifications, e.g., al-Bâra and Afamiya (formerly Apamea). In general, the sizeable towns that had survived still possessed their original defences, most of them dating from the era of Byzantine sovereignty. These were simple curtain walls, thickly studded with towers and often reinforced with ditches or light outworks. One or two towns (e.g., Aleppo) boasted specially reinforced citadels of ancient date or had acquired them during the Byzantine-Arab wars (e.g., Antioch, in 975).

In all but a few instances, original fortifications were not augmented by their new masters after the Arab conquest. New defences had been constructed only in one or two Palestinian sea-ports (Acre, Ascalon, Caesarea) or in areas near the Byzantine-Arab border, where there was a constant threat of attack. From the beginning of the 10th century onwards, since the walls of many older settlements were difficult to defend, a number of new fortresses had been erected in their vicinity by the Byzantines and, more especially, by local native rulers. What differentiated these strongholds from earlier Byzantine fortresses was their secluded position on inaccessible heights and the asymmetrical lay-out of their perimeter walls, which moulded themselves to the terrain. Their combination of defensible seignorial residence and small fortified settlement fully entitles them to be regarded as castles in the medieval sense (e.g., Sahyûn-Argyrokastron). Shortly afterwards, in the 11th century, similar buildings of a type better adapted to the security requirements of the period were evolved as fortified residences by the petty Armenian princes who controlled the broad expanse of highlands between the Taurus and the Euphrates. It was near them, in the newly established County of Edessa, that the Franks settled.

Just as Baldwin had remained in Edessa, so Bohemond stayed behind at Antioch with his Normans when, after a lengthy interval, the Crusader army finally resumed its march on Jerusalem during the spring of 1099. Pausing only to deal with one or two fortified towns, the knights reached the Holy City on 7 June 1099. After two abortive assaults, they settled down to build the requisite siege-engines. On 15 July, one of their large siege-towers was successfully manoeuvred close enough to the walls to enable Duke Godfrey's knights to storm the battlements after a fierce struggle and go on from there to occupy the city. Jerusalem fell, and the goal of more than three years' campaigning had finally been attained.

CONQUEST OF THE HOLY LAND 1100-1143

Within a few weeks of the capture of the Holy City and the founding of the Kingdom of Jerusalem, an event took place which posed the problem of how to retain and consolidate what had already been won. A strong Egyptian army dispatched by the Fatimid caliphs and commanded by the Vizier al-Afdal advanced from Egypt with the object of recapturing the lost city. In August 1099 the Egyptians were routed near Ascalon, a defeat which provisionally consolidated the Franks' hold on Jerusalem and guaranteed the extension of their sphere of control. Bohemond's nephew Tancred, originally installed as Prince of Galilee by Godfrey of Bouillon, began by conquering the area north of Jerusalem, long a bone of contention between the Egyptian Fatimids and the Seljuk lords of Damascus. The primary objectives of Godfrey (d. 1100) and his successor Baldwin I were the coastal towns occupied by the Egyptians. Jaffa, Arsûf, Caesarea, Acre (St Jean d'Acre), Beirut and Saidâ fell into Frankish hands in quick succession during the decade 1100-1110, while the two strong sea-fortresses of Tyre and Ascalon, which could not be taken without naval support, were sealed off by the erection of small block-forts. Now that the fertile coastal strip had been brought under Frankish control within a few short years, King Baldwin I turned his attention to the east. In 1115 he invaded eastern Jordan, and in the following year, basing his advance on the newly constructed fortress of Montreal (aš-Šôbak), he pushed onwards to the Red Sea, where he fortified the harbour of Ailat and erected a small castle on the outlying Ile de Graye.

While the first two Frankish rulers had concentrated primarily upon enlarging their domains in Palestine, Baldwin II, who became King of Jerusalem in 1118, Regent of Antioch in 1119 and Regent of Edessa in 1122, transferred the focus of Frankish-Islamic rivalry to the north-east of the country, where it remained for some decades. Progress was also made further south, however. In 1124, with the assistance of a Venetian fleet, Baldwin succeeded in capturing Tyre, which had been under siege for years, and a short while later he acquired the powerful fortress of Paneas (Qal'at Subeibe) from the Ismaelites. Together with the fortresses constructed by Baldwin I – Safed (1102) and Le Toron (1104) – Paneas served, after extensive improvement, to protect the Damascus flank of the kingdom's northern border.

In Palestine, the Kingdom of Jerusalem developed in the course of thirty years into a power which was strictly administered according to medieval feudal law and controlled substantial tracts of territory. Meanwhile, the Frankish princes resident in Lebanon and Syria had greatly augmented their domains at the expense of the numerous and perpetually disunited emirates in their neighbourhood. In 1102, proceeding from the small fortified harbour of Tortosa, Count Raymond of Toulouse conquered the fertile Lebanese coastal region, including the port of Giblet, and occupied parts of the adjoining highlands in the east. In 1103 he vigorously embarked on the siege of Tripoli by building the small block-fort of Mons Peregrinus. After his death in 1105 his successors maintained the blockade until the city fell in 1109. Subsequently, basing their operations on the small fortress of Montferrand, built in 1115, and on Rafaniya, captured from the Arabs at about the same time, they launched fierce attacks on the possessions of the Seljuk Atâbegs of Damascus and the Emirs of Homs and Hamâ.

The development of the two northernmost Frankish states was less consistent. After Bohemond had been severely defeated at Harrân, his nephew Tancred ruled the principality from 1100 until 1112. He captured the important harbour of Lattaqia (La Liche) from the Byzantines in 1102, conquered new territory in the north while campaigning against the Danishmend Turks, and, after a series of fluctuating battles with the Seljuk rulers of Aleppo, extended his sovereignty eastwards across the Orontes. These initial successes against largely disunited local Turkish princes were followed by the appearance of a determined and power-ful adversary in the person of the Ortokid prince Il-Ghâzi, who virtually annihilated the Norman army at the gory battle of the Ager Sanguinis in 1119, thus putting paid to further expansion for the time being. The position of the two Frankish petty states became genuinely precarious when, in 1128, the able Atâbeg of Mossul, Imâd ad-dîn Zengî, gained possession of the important city of Aleppo and later of the emirates of Homs and Hamâ. Having at first concentrated on augmenting his Mesopotamian possessions, he later turned, from 1135 onwards, against his Christian foes in the west. Zengî was held in check for a short time in 1137-8 by the intervention of Emperor John II Comnenus of Byzantium, but thereafter resumed his attacks with undiminished vigour. These were directed not only against the Franks but also against the Seljuk rulers of Damascus, who promptly joined forces with the former.

Petty jealousies among the Seljuk princes temporarily compelled the Atâbeg to turn his attention to his eastern possessions, thereby giving the Franks a breathing-space which King Fulk of Jerusalem, formerly Count of Anjou, used to strengthen the borders of his realm. His treaty with Damascus had regained him the fortress of Paneas, which had been lost in the interim, and he began to improve the neighbouring castle of Safed shortly afterwards. Belvoir, another castle situated somewhat further south, was rebuilt at about the same time. To protect his southern borders against constant incursions by the Egyptian garrison at Ascalon, Fulk had previously built the small castle of Bethgibelin (1137), near which he later built Blanchegarde and Ibelin (1141-2). He also commissioned his vassal Payen le Bouteiller to construct the powerful fortress of Kerak (1142) in Transjordan, which had been conquered by his predecessors.

In contrast to the older fortifications which the Franks had taken over and partly rebuilt, the newly constructed castles were, first and foremost, offensive bases designed to function

JERUSALEM

either as depots for the Frankish besiegers of the large coastal fortresses or as spring-boards for new expeditions and lightning raids into enemy territory. Consequently, most of them were sited in well-protected and strategically important positions near major caravan routes or beside approach roads to large towns, where they would afford the best possible view of the surrounding terrain. Visual contact with neighbouring fortresses was also important (e.g., at Safita and Arima), but the main principle of the new castles, as of those that had been built by Byzantines and Arab emirs in the 10th and 11th centuries, was that they should conform to the local topography and exploit the natural advantages of their mountainous surroundings as skilfully as possible. A specially reinforced keep or donjon was built on the spot which afforded the best natural protection, while the lower and generally more spacious part of a fortress was enclosed by lighter defences. The walls and towers of these Frankish castles, most of them constructed of good stonework, were almost invariably stronger than those of earlier Byzantine and Arab fortresses. No emergence of a standard type can be observed among these castles in the Palestinian highlands, whereas contemporary castles in the flat coastal regions do conform to a fixed type which was clearly based on Norman tradition and probably represented the Crusaders' major contribution to the development of military architecture in the Levant. As in Northern France and the South of England, these castles consisted of an extremely strong, multi-storeyed tower (donjon), enclosed by a single rectangular curtain wall, often reinforced with corner-towers, and a wide ditch or fosse (e.g., *inter alia*, Blanchegarde, Safita and Qal'at Yahmûr). In larger castles (e.g., Sahyûn) donjons of this type were frequently constructed so as to reinforce particularly vulnerable points. The donjon does not occur in Byzantine and rarely in later Armenian fortifications. In Roman times, strong defensive towers were built for a brief period only and in a limited area of Northern Syria, where they formed strong-points in the local *limes* system. Also in evidence as early as the 5th century A. D. were prototypes of the machicolated gallery which became so widespread during the Middle Ages.

In addition to these offensive bases, most of which occupied outlying positions, numerous Frankish fortresses came into being on the coastal strip and the western slopes of the mountains bordering it. In the hinterland, a large number of seigneurs, great and small, gradually established fixed abodes, often on previously fortified sites which they had expropriated from Arab emirs by force of arms or stratagem (e.g., Krak, Sahyûn and Margat). Little is known of the original lay-out and appearance of these strongholds because most of the castles which were built by vassals towards the end of the 12th century, or in the 13th century at latest, passed later into the possession of the powerful knightly orders and underwent radical rebuilding and alteration as a result.

The original function of these orders – the Order of St John, which had been in existence since before the capture of Jerusalem and was constituted a knightly order early in the 12th century, and the newly established Order of the Temple, founded in 1120 by Hugues de Payen – was to protect travelling pilgrims and tend them if they fell sick, but this function was soon overshadowed by the knightly obligation to wage war against the Infidel. As early as 1137, King Fulk entrusted the Knights of St John, or Hospitallers, with the castle of Bethgibelin – newly constructed on their own land – as a base from which to guard and defend the frontier.

BALANCE OF POWER 1143-1187

When King Fulk died in 1143, the four Crusader states had reached the limit of their expansion. In the following year, their northern corner-stone crumbled under the impact of a surprise attack by Atâbeg Zengî. Taking advantage of the weakened state of the Kingdom of Jerusalem, which was now under the regency of Queen Melisende, he suddenly invaded the County of Edessa, took the capital after a brief siege, and occupied half the county. He was only prevented from exploiting his success to the full by unrest in his native Mosul. Although optimism was aroused by Zengî's assassination and the short-lived reoccupation of Edessa by Frankish-Armenian forces, it soon became clear that the Frankish states had gained a still more dangerous adversary in the Atâbeg's son, Nûr ad-dîn.

Even graver than the loss of these rich northern territories was the disastrous failure of the Second Crusade, which had been inspired by news of the loss of Edessa. Both sections of the German army under Emperor Conrad III and Bishop Otto of Freising were annihilated by the Seljuks at Dorylaeum and Laodicea, while the French army under King Louis VII suffered such heavy losses in the passes of the Taurus mountains and outside Antalya, that only meagre remnants of the expeditionary force reached the Holy Land in 1148. For various reasons, instead of attacking their most dangerous foe, Nûr ad-dîn of Aleppo, the Crusaders launched an abortive assault on Damascus, which had hitherto been on friendly terms with the Franks. However, the real failure of this Crusade consisted less in political blunders and military defeats than in the disagreements which arose with Byzantium, in the open estrangement between the newly arrived Crusaders and the Franks who had been resident in the country for a generation, and, above all, in the serious blow which the Franks' military prestige had sustained in the eyes of their Muslim adversaries. Shortly after the luckless Crusaders' departure, Nûr ad-dîn invaded the Principality of Antioch, inflicting several bloody defeats on the Franks and depriving them, by 1149, of all their domains to the east of the Orontes. Taking advantage of the confusion prevailing among the Franks, Sultan Mas'ûd of Konya simultaneously seized those areas of the County of Edessa which still remained in Frankish hands. The Principality and Antioch itself were saved by the prompt intervention of King Baldwin III, but the extensive eastern territories and the County of Edessa were lost for good.

In 1154, although Baldwin had concluded a new treaty of alliance with the rulers of Damascus and pursued a policy designed to prevent the Zengid from encroaching on the city, Nûr ad-dîn managed after several unsuccessful attempts to gain control of the Syrian capital, thereby swaying the balance of power decisively in his favour. Baldwin had also scored a major triumph, however. In 1153, after beleaguering it for years, the Franks finally captured Ascalon, the large sea-port which constituted the Egyptians' most important stronghold in Palestine. Damage sustained by both sides in the severe earthquake of 1157 necessitated extensive reconstruction work and so conduced a temporary lull. At the same time, Nûr ad-dîn's spirit of enterprise was further dampened by the emergence of Emperor Manuel Comnenus, who, having defeated the Sultan of Konya and the Armenians in Cilicia, entered Antioch in triumph in 1158. Apart from a brief foray against Aleppo, however, the Emperor did nothing to diminish substantially the power of the Franks' major foe.

While Nûr ad-dîn's strength increased year by year in Syria, that of the Fatimid caliphate in Egypt declined steadily. After Baldwin III's untimely death in 1162, his successor, Amalric I, assessed the situation correctly and turned his attentions to Egypt. His aim was to wean it from the influence of the dreaded Zengid by imposing a form of Frankish protectorate, continuing disunity among the Franks' Islamic neighbours being the only long-term guarantee of the Frankish kingdom's survival. The Franks' first expedition to Egypt ended in failure. Their second brought them face to face with a Syrian army commanded by the able general Šîrkûh. Meanwhile, Nûr ad-dîn seized the opportunity to attack in Syria, where he occupied the important castles of Paneas and Hârim, recently recaptured by the Franks. In 1167 war broke out again in Egypt. In face of a renewed attack by the Syrian army under Šîrkûh, the Egyptians again solicited aid from King Amalric, who fought Šîrkûh with varying success in the area between Alexandria and Middle Egypt. Although the outcome was not decisive, the Egyptians had once more succeeded in asserting their independence – if only under Frankish protection. In 1168, in contravention of treaties concluded with the Egyptians and of firm plans – already agreed with Emperor Manuel of Byzantium – for a joint expedition in the following year, Amalric yielded to pressure from his barons and marched into Egypt yet again. His advance on Cairo not only failed to gain him any notable successes but finally drove the terrified Egyptians into his chief enemy's camp. Despite the schism existing between the two Islamic powers – the Fatimid Egyptians were Shiites and the Syrians Sunnites – Šîrkûh assumed power in Cairo. When he died a few months later, his place was taken by his nephew Ṣalâḥ ed-dîn (the Saladin of Frankish chronicles), who soon managed to gain control of the country.

With their two Islamic neighbours united under a single powerful ruler, the Franks found themselves menaced by the danger of a war on two fronts. Fortunately for them, however, relations between Saladin and his former master, Nûr ad-dîn, rapidly deteriorated. Furthermore, Syria was devastated by another earthquake in 1170, and both camps once more busied themselves with large-scale reconstruction work. The shift in the balance of power and the totally changed strategic situation produced distinct changes in the lay-out and appearance of fortifications. Early in the 12th century, rival Syrian emirs had been hard put to it to raise sufficient funds to improve their defences. As a result, they were almost universally compelled to repair out-of-date strongholds or modify suitable buildings of earlier date for purposes

SAHYUN

of defence (e.g., by converting the Roman theatre at Bosra into a citadel and transforming the temple precincts at Ba'albek into a fortress). From the middle of the 12th century onwards, now that their dissipated energies had been canalized by a series of powerful rulers, the Muslims, too, could begin to build stronger fortresses (e.g., Sheizar) and even establish offensive bases such as the castle of Qal'at 'Ajlûn, erected opposite Belvoir in 1184.

In proportion as the tide of Frankish expansion was checked and, from the middle of the 12th century, decisively reversed by growing Muslim strength, so Frankish fortifications lost their predominantly offensive role and assumed an increasingly defensive character – without, however, undergoing any fundamental change in design. Both in the border areas and, more especially, in the hinterland, castles and walled towns of the Frankish period had to be considerably strengthened. A characteristic example of this is the fortress of Sahyûn, which was rebuilt sometime during the second third of the 12th century. Vulnerable flanks were reinforced with stout walls and strong towers to render them proof against the enemy's improved siegecraft. From the middle of the century onwards, however, since very few of the castles' owners or the feudal seigneurs occupying them were in a position to foot the bill for urgent improvements or repairs necessitated by earthquakes, more and more castles passed into the possession of the knightly orders. The knights had amassed great wealth and considerable political power in the course of the years. Having established their headquarters at Tortosa between 1160 and 1170, the Templars had tightened their hold on the country surrounding the town by building a series of small but well-fortified strongholds, among them Arima and Chastel-Blanc/Safita. The Hospitallers, too, had begun to rebuild a number of powerful fortresses, notably Krak des Chevaliers (owned by their order since 1142) and Margat, acquired by the Knights in 1186.

When Nûr ad-dîn died in 1174, serious fighting broke out in the Islamic camp over the right of succession. The Franks might well have turned this to their advantage had not King Amalric also died unexpectedly a few months later. As it was, the Franks themselves fell to squabbling over the regency of thirteen-year-old Baldwin IV, and the only person to profit from the situation was Saladin, who assumed the overlordship of Damascus from Cairo without Frankish interference. His simultaneous attempt to annex Northern Syria went awry because Count Raymond III of Tripoli intervened in favour of the Zengids of Aleppo and the Shiite Ismaelites also ranged themselves against him. Persian in origin and commonly known as 'Assassins', this sect did not wield any great military power, but its tightly knit religio-political structure made it a factor to be reckoned with in contemporary disputes. After being expelled from Damascus in 1129, its adherents had settled in the inaccessible valleys of the Nûsairî mountains, a no man's land situated between Frank and Muslim in south-west Syria. Here they held a number of small but strong and well-protected fortresses (e.g., Masyâf, Qadmûs, Abu Qubeis, El-Kahf and Olleiqa) which they retained until the close of the 13th century.

Saladin continued his attempts to weld Nûr ad-dîn's dominions together under his leadership during the years that followed, neglecting no opportunity to invade Frankish territory in the process. Meanwhile, the Frankish camp witnessed a rapid decline in royal authority during the reign of Baldwin IV, although the young and leprous king did initially achieve a few minor successes. Having defeated Saladin at Montgisart in 1177, he seized the opportunity to reinforce his northern frontier, which had been weakened by the loss of Paneas, by building two new castles, Hûnîn (Château-Neuf) and Le Chastellet. Despite the heroic defence put up by its Templar garrison, Le Chastellet was captured and destroyed by Saladin in the following year.

Young Baldwin's days were clearly numbered. As time passed, it became increasingly apparent that he no longer possessed the strength to subordinate the often conflicting interests of feudal lords, knightly orders and churchmen to a common objective. In 1177, Bohemond III of Antioch marched against the Zengids of Aleppo, who were kept in power by the Franks, and attacked the fortress of Hârim with the assistance of Flemish Crusaders. He later came into conflict with his liege lord and Armenian neighbours by overtly committing adultery. Reynald of Châtillon, who had acquired Frankish Transjordan by marriage after his release from Arab captivity, violated peace treaties concluded between Baldwin and Saladin by ambushing Muslim caravans and waging a piratical war in the Red Sea on his own initiative. Far graver than these cases of insubordination by individual princes, however, was the ruthless nepotism practised by the court camarilla at Jerusalem under the leadership of the ambitious queen mother, who, heedless of the extremely critical situation and in defiance of the Frankish barons and the king himself, sponsored Guy of Lusignan – an incompetent – as successor to Baldwin's throne. With the death of Emperor Manuel Comnenus in 1180, one of the Franks' mainstays disappeared, because Manuel's successor did not perpetuate his policy of friendship towards them. On the Muslim side, Saladin succeeded during 1182-3 in incorporating large tracts of Northern Syria in his realm, together with Aleppo, so long a focus of strife. His dominions now extended from Cyrenaica to the Tigris, and the Franks had never before been confronted by a ruler of such power and ability.

HATTÎN 1187

At the end of 1186, despite the precarious nature of the situation and the truce which still reigned between the two sides, Reynald of Châtillon attacked another large Muslim caravan and refused to make restitution. This renewed challenge to Saladin rendered war inevitable. The Sultan mustered a huge army in the Haurân, crossed the Jordan, and, after a preliminary cavalry success, annihilated the Frankish army at Hattîn on 4 July 1187. Almost every member of the Frankish nobility fell in battle or was taken prisoner. Promptly following up this triumph, Saladin divided his forces and marched on the almost undefended sea-ports, capturing Acre, Jaffa and Beirut within a few days. In September, having occupied large areas of the Frankish hinterland, he advanced on Jerusalem and compelled it to surrender after barely a fortnight's stubborn resistance. He continued his triumphal progress during the ensuing twelve months, operating partly against the strongholds still in Frankish hands but principally against the sea-ports of Lebanon and Syria. Tripoli and Tortosa held out, but Saidâ, Giblet, Gabala and La Liche (Lattaqia) fell into Saladin's hands, together with the inland fortresses of Sahyûn, Balatunus, Burzey and, further to the north, Bağras and Trapesac. Thanks to the bravery of their garrisons, some of the larger castles in the south – Beaufort Belvoir, Safad Kerak and Montreal – managed to hold out for a considerable time, but were starved into submission during the winter of 1188-9.

Discounting these few instances, the main reason why so many powerful fortresses surrendered quickly was not hunger but lack of able-bodied men and the unlikelihood of relief, not to mention the universal dismay engendered by the débâcle at Hattîn. Thus, the Sultan had an easy task with many Frankish strongholds. If the gates were not thrown open voluntarily, he often managed to storm the ill-defended walls at the first assault. Even so, a number of castles did not fall until they had been formally besieged. Depending on circumstances, their walls had to be either undermined or breached by bombardment with heavy catapults (mangonels) so that the besiegers could storm the gap. The Arabs favoured the former method, which entailed sapping likely sections of wall or exposed points in the enemy defences. The subterranean shafts were then shored up with stout balks of dry timber and packed with combustible material, so that they collapsed when fired, usually bringing down a large section of wall with them. This was how Saladin had captured the newly-built Templar fortress of Le Chastellet in 1179, and he now proceeded to take the fortified harbour of La Liche (Lattaqia) in the same way. When sapping was impracticable because of groundwater close beneath the surface, rocky subsoil or topographical conditions, the besiegers had to try to bring down walls by bombarding them with heavy stones. Here, however, the defenders' opportunities for counter-measures were greater, since they could impede the enemy by conducting vigorous sorties or destroying his siege-engines with their own mangonels and ballistae. Although the Templars succeeded in holding Tortosa, their main stronghold, by these means, Saladin managed to take the castles of Trapesac and Šugr-Bakas, hitherto regarded as impregnable, by employing heavy catapults.

Less serviceable at this period were older siege-engines of the type which the Crusaders had used on Jerusalem in 1099, e.g., the ram, bore and siege-tower, whose use generally demanded more time and – in the case of the helepole or mobile siege-tower – almost level ground.

It should be mentioned that treachery also contributed to Saladin's swift and triumphal progress (as at Burzey), and that even the best-constructed castle occasionally had unguarded crannies through which an alert and skilful besieger could gain access to the interior without undue difficulty. It was at just such an unguarded spot that the attackers penetrated the almost impregnable castle of Sahyûn after a brief siege and bombardment, and captured it with a minimum of fighting.

SHEÎZAR

THE KINGDOM OF ACRE 1191-1291

After Saladin had campaigned in Frankish territory for a year, practically the entire kingdom of Jerusalem was lost. Further north the Franks still held Antioch and Tripoli, as well as sea ports like Tyre and major strongholds like Krak, Margat and Safita. The reconquest of the lost lands could only be undertaken from bases such as these, notably Tyre, whose defence had been conducted with vigour and determination by Conrad of Montferrat, who had reached there at the eleventh hour. Meanwhile, remnants of the Frankish army commanded by King Guy of Lusignan, who had since been released from captivity, began to lay siege to Acre. Still under the impact of the disaster at Hattîn, the Pope pronounced in favour of a new Crusade in the West. A Norman fleet appeared at Tripoli as early as 1187, but Emperor Frederick I (Barbarossa) was the first to lead a large army eastwards by the overland route. The Germans fought their way through Seljuk-controlled Asia Minor with heavy losses during the summer of 1190, but the emperor's tragic death in the Calycadnus virtually dispersed the army just before it reached its destination. Kings Philip of France and Richard Cœur de Lion of England set out with their armies by sea a short while later. During his journey Richard conquered the rich island of Cyprus within a few weeks. In 1191, after the arrival of these two powerful armies, the long-beleaguered city of Acre was quickly taken and remained the capital of the Frankish dominions for a full century.

Richard at once advanced southwards along the coast and inflicted a severe defeat on Saladin at Arsûf. Meanwhile, in Acre, another violent dispute broke out over the monarchy. In place of the unpopular Guy of Lusignan, the barons chose Conrad of Montferrat, a much more able man who was succeeded, after his mysterious assassination, by Count Henry of Champagne. Guy was consoled with the Kingdom of Cyprus. In spite of his several military successes against Saladin, Richard Coeur de Lion did not manage to launch a decisive attack against Jerusalem. News from home eventually prompted him to make peace with Saladin, and in the autumn of 1192 he returned to Europe with a substantial proportion of the Crusader army.

This peace treaty held out the prospect of a new balance of power between the two unequal adversaries. When Saladin died in the following year, 1193, a dispute over the right of succession broke out between his sons and brother despite the foresight and wisdom of the Sultan's political testament. This afforded King Henry an opportunity to strengthen the Frankish position, and he skilfully and prudently made full use of it. He managed to restore Giblet to its former owner without recourse to arms, maintained good relations with the 'Old Man of the Mountain', as the head of the Ismaelite Assassins was known, and mediated in the dispute that had long been raging between King Leo II of Armenia and Bohemond III of Antioch. He was shrewd enough to settle his differences with the new Kingdom of Cyprus, too, with the result that Amalric of Lusignan, who was elected king after Henry's death in 1197, united the thrones of Jerusalem and Cyprus in his own person. Amalric II was as prudent and adroit a politician as his predecessor. By recapturing Beirut in 1197 with the aid of German and Brabantine knights, he succeeded in restoring overland communication between Tripoli and Acre, *de facto* capital of the newly reconstituted Kingdom of Jerusalem.

In the West, a great new Fourth Crusade was gathering at the powerful insistence of Pope Innocent III. Under the influence of Venice, however, it soon turned against Byzantium and, by capturing the imperial city of Constantinople in 1204, laid the foundations of a new Latin empire in the east. Originally intended to buttress the Franks' precarious position in the Holy Land, this Crusade ultimately had the opposite effect, not only because it failed to bring Palestine the fresh reinforcements which were so urgently needed there but also because it tapped the existing man-power of the threatened area. Thanks, however, to the moderate policies of its kings and the absence of a dominant leader on the Arab side, the small Frankish state was able to make further progress. In 1204 Amalric II concluded a new peace treaty with Sultan Malik al-'Adil, Saladin's brother and successor, under the terms of which he regained former Frankish possessions which included Saidâ and Jaffa. This truce remained in force throughout the regency of John of Ibelin (1205-10) and during the early years of King John of Brienne's reign, disturbed only by isolated raids into Ayyubid territory by restless knights. On the other hand, relations between the small Principality of Antioch and the Kingdom of Armenia became severely strained by the dispute over who was to succeed Bohemond III, and tension was not relieved until Bohemond IV assumed power in 1219.

Meanwhile, in 1217, the first units of the Fifth Crusade had landed in Palestine. One contingent headed by King Andrew II of Hungary made weak and ill-led sorties against Paneas and another castle which had recently been erected on Mount Tabor by the Arabs. For the rest, the army was employed in strengthening the defences of Caesarea and constructing the powerful Templar fortress of Chastel Pèlerin. It was not until 1218 that the main army, in conjunction with the Kingdom's forces, undertook a large-scale invasion of Egypt, main-spring of Ayyubid power. The fortress of Damietta fell into Frankish hands in 1219, after a long siege. Repeated proposals by Sultan Malik al-Kâmil that Damietta should be traded for Jerusalem and large areas of Palestine were most surprisingly rejected by Cardinal Pelagius, Papal Legate and commander of the expedition, who had arrived on the scene belatedly. In 1221, against the advice of the Frankish barons, he launched a drive on Cairo, but was brought to a standstill outside the stoutly built fortress of Mansûra. The army was only saved after all its acquisitions had been handed back and an eight-year truce signed with the Sultan.

In 1225, hoping to find an even mightier defender of the Holy Land, John of Brienne – backed by Pope Honorius III – married his young daughter Isabelle to Emperor Frederick II, an ambitious ruler whose involvement introduced factors with which the '*Poulains*', as Frankish settlers in the Levant were known, had not had to deal before. Although the Pope urged Frederick to launch his long-vowed Crusade without delay, the Emperor continued to conduct long-range negotiations with the quarrelling Islamic factions and confined himself to dispatching a small advance party, which spent the intervening period – almost a full year –

in improving the defences of Caesarea and Saidâ and in rebuilding the dilapidated castle of Montfort for the benefit of the newly created Teutonic Order (1198). Frederick eventually set forth in 1228, but no sooner had he landed in Cyprus than he became embroiled in the internal disputes of the Frankish nobility and incurred the hostility of the Ibelin party. After so many years of independence, this large and powerful group of French noblemen was understandably reluctant to submit to strict and, by contemporary standards, questionable royal authority.

Shortly after his arrival in Palestine, Frederick II was able to occupy the Holy Places under the terms of his treaty with the Ayyubid Sultan, Malik al-Kâmil. Jerusalem, Bethlehem and Nazareth were restored to Frankish ownership in 1229, an important and tangible achievement on the Emperor's part, even though it was based not on feats of arms but on his own political expertise and on a joint endeavour by both sides to substitute toleration for the religious fanaticism of yore. Although Frederick made himself King of Jerusalem in the Church of the Holy Sepulchre, the majority of Frankish nobles still opposed him. His party was challenged as soon as he departed, and forces sent by him were ultimately expelled from Palestine and Cyprus after years of civil war. The monarchy, which was the sole force that could still have united and controlled the conflicting trends in the Frankish Levant, finally collapsed. The fact that further Frankish successes of a minor nature were recorded during this period (e.g., the reoccupation of Safed, Beaufort and Tiberias) was attributable solely to the dissension that prevailed between the two well-matched Islamic factions after Sultan Malik al-Kâmil's death. As soon as one of these feuding groups gained ascendancy over the other, the Franks were bound to suffer severe losses. This was how, after an invasion by the Khwarezmian allies of the Egyptian party, the Holy City and the surrounding area came to be lost again in 1244 – this time for good.

Reports that Jerusalem had been lost yet again at once impelled the West to prepare for another Crusade, the sixth, but it was 1248 before the commander of the expedition, King Louis IX of France (Saint Louis) could set out with his army, by which time the Franks had also lost Tiberias and the stronghold of Ascalon. Correctly gauging that, in view of the weakness of the Ayyubid sultanate, it would be easier to defeat the enemy on his home ground, Louis directed his attack against Egypt. The French king landed at Damietta in 1249 and took the place by storm at the first attempt. Flushed with enthusiasm by their swift success and doubtless prejudiced against the diplomatic tactics which had been employed by Emperor Frederick II, the Crusaders committed the same blunder as had King Amalric I and Cardinal Pelagius. Instead of accepting the Ayyubid Sultan's offer to exchange Damietta for Jerusalem and Galilee, King Louis marched on Cairo. While en route, the army was halted in its tracks by Mamelukes at Mansûra, and in April 1250, weakened by this defeat and a severe typhus epidemic, it was forced to surrender with Louis at its head. The release of the French king and his sadly depleted forces was only secured after the payment of an immense indemnity and the return of Damietta. They then embarked for Acre, where Louis remained for another four years. Although Emperor Conrad IV was the titular King of

KRAK DES CHEVALIERS

Jerusalem, Louis assumed the regency during his sojourn in Palestine without arousing opposition in any quarter. He improved the defences of Acre, Saidâ, Caesarea and Jaffa, reorganized the country, got trade moving again, and tried, ultimately without success, to play off the two enemy camps – the Egyptian Mamelukes and the Ayyubid rulers of Damascus – against each other for the benefit of the Frankish states.

Both because of and despite the Franks' political and military weakness, this period simultaneously witnessed the acme and end of Frankish fortification in the Levant. It produced substantial portions of the castles that survive today and, more especially, the bulk of the major town fortifications, which underwent improvement from about the middle of the 13th century onwards. The latter reveal a manifest change in the social structure of the Frankish state. Originally, towns were fortified with simple perimeter walls merely to an extent which would render them defensible against surprise attack. The defences of, say, Tortosa and Giblet demonstrate that only the citadels were made strong enough to withstand formal siege. Owing to the increasing density of population in the Frankish coastal towns which constituted the main seats of spiritual and secular power and, above all, to their growing importance as centres of economic life and commercial traffic, it was inevitable that, as the threat to coast and hinterland mounted, they should be better constructed and more heavily fortified than had been the practice hitherto.

Little enough has survived of these fortifications, it is true. Only excavation can enhance our knowledge of them in the towns which were devastated and abandoned after the Franks had been expelled (Ascalon, Arsûf, Caesarea, Tripoli), while in those that still existed after 1291 (Acre, Tyre, Saidâ, Beirut) all but meagre remnants of the obsolete, superfluous and inconvenient town walls were demolished in more recent times. Nevertheless, these isolated fragments, coupled with contemporary descriptions, enable us to deduce that parts of such fortifications must have been extremely strong. The triple walls erected on the inland flank of Tyre were particularly famous, as were the town fortifications of Acre, which consisted throughout their entire length of a double wall guarded by towers. The perimeter walls enclosing these cities were reinforced with low bastions or towers (usually rectangular) situated at more or less regular intervals (90-120 feet), the latter being determined by the range of bows and missiles. In front of them lay wide ditches, often filled with water, and – sometimes – simple outworks. Town gates were heavily fortified as a rule, though they seldom displayed the structural elaboration of citadel and castle gate-houses. They were generally guarded by adjacent towers, and access to the interior was protected by one or more right-angled bends – often, too, by a series of gate-chambers which could be sealed off and raked with overhead or enfilading fire.

All harbours were provided with special defence installations. Because of the modest size of sea-going vessels in those days, most harbours were smallish bays, often sheltered by broad reefs of rock but usually given the additional protection of moles. At the extremities of the reefs or moles enclosing the entrance stood harbour-forts or strong towers between which, in accordance with ancient practice, were stretched the iron chains that functioned as booms.

Also sited here were catapults or ballistae for repelling hostile ships (harbour-forts at Saidâ and Giblet; block-towers at Acre, Beirut, Lattaqia and elsewhere). A harbour was generally separated from the town by walls. Quays were very rare, and ships were normally beached on the flat sandy shore or anchored in the harbour.

In constructing these strong town fortifications, the Franks adopted a long-established form of Levantine architecture which the differently constituted social structure of their country had so far enabled them to disregard. Meanwhile, the building of castles continued to develop in the direction which had been taken since the middle of the 12th century, when there was a transition from lightly fortified offensive bases to more heavily fortified defensive strongpoints; that is to say, there was a consistent trend towards reinforcing the defensive capabilities of individual fortresses. Just as the medieval technique of fortification had hitherto produced virtually no important innovations which might have distinguished it from that of the ancient world, so the Franks now confined themselves to reduplicating elements already in use; in other words, they simply increased the number of artificial hazards or boosted the dimensions of traditional architectural features. Curtain-walls, the backbone of any defensive system, were reinforced against bombardment, sapping and earthquakes by augmenting the thickness of masonry, building tapering walls (talus) after arab customs and putting ancient columns as bonds into the walls. At the same time, their defensive strength was substantially enhanced by increasing the number of embrasures in them, installing tiers of superimposed defensive galleries pierced with loopholes, and building projecting machicolated galleries. Towers, which were usually rectangular but which sometimes adopted a semicircular shape from the early 13th century onwards, possibly under Armenian influence, were correspondingly strengthened and modified so as to enfilade the neighbouring curtain-walls and thereby be able to contribute to their defence.

Military architects paid particular attention to the building of gates, although contemporary accounts inform us that these seldom came under direct attack by besiegers, who invariably concentrated on the long curtain-walls. The requisite strengthening of gates was achieved not only by reinforcing walls and barriers (portcullis, drawbridge, gate panels, etc.) and increasing the number of enfilading points in the interior, but by multiplying artificial hazards in such a way that they were skilfully adapted to the terrain and could be enfiladed from well-protected galleries. On the principle that individual features should be reduplicated, builders of new castles abandoned single curtain-walls in favour of double walls with open forecourts running between them (Krak, Margat), increased the number of towers and ditches, or constructed outworks from which catapults of limited range could be kept at a safe distance from the main fortifications. To sum up, one might describe the prevailing trend as an attempt on the part of defenders to husband man-power by multiplying and strengthening defensive barriers, i.e., to substitute material for men so as to coerce besiegers into a correspondingly greater expenditure of siege equipment and man-power. The full extent of the influence exerted on the subsequent development of military architecture throughout Western Europe by this latter evolutionary phase in the Levant cannot yet be gauged, but it is certain that medieval military architecture both in France and Italy – especially Southern Italy under Hohenstaufen rule – derived important stimuli from the Holy Land.

King Louis IX's departure from Palestine in 1254, after four years in the country, signalled the end of Western Europe's final attempt to maintain its possessions in the Levant. Old feuds promptly flared up again, and the traditional hostility between Venice, Genoa and Pisa gave rise to the disastrous and bloody civil war known as the War of St Saba (1256-8), during which the whole of Syria eventually took sides with one or other of the warring factions. The individual Frankish power-groups – they could no longer be termed a kingdom – were equally incapable of agreeing on a common foreign policy. While Bohemond VI of Antioch-Tripoli co-operated with King Hethum I of Armenia in backing the Christian Mongol leader Kitbuga during the large-scale Mongol invasion of 1260, the barons in Palestine supported the Mameluke Sultan Baibars, whose victory over the Mongols at 'Ain Ǧalût gained him that part of Syria which had hitherto been in Ayyubid hands.

The petty Frankish states were once again confronted by a united Muslim bloc, but this time they were rent by internal strife and face to face with an adversary who was harsh to the point of brutality and grimly determined to annihilate his Christian foes once and for all. Proceeding methodically, Sultan Baibars stripped the Franks of one stronghold after another during the years 1261-72, and reports of a new (seventh) Crusade in 1270 afforded them little relief. Caesarea and Arsûf fell in 1265, the newly reconstructed Templar fortress of Safed in 1266, Jaffa, Beaufort, Antioch and its neighbouring castles in 1268, Chastel-Blanc, Akkar and the mighty Krak des Chevaliers in 1271, and Montfort shortly thereafter. The remainder of the country was saved by a humiliating peace treaty signed in 1272. Although strife between rival claimants for Baibars' throne afforded the Franks another brief respite after his murder in 1277, the new sultan, Qala'ûn, who was brought to power by the Syrian army, had so effectively consolidated his authority by 1280 that he, too, was able to begin operations against the disunited Franks, whom he skilfully played off against one another. In 1285 the Sultan captured the stronghold of Margat, in 1289 Tripoli and the last remaining Antiochene possessions. In 1291, after a bitter struggle, Acre fell to Qala'ûn's son, al-Ašraf Khalîl. The Franks abandoned the few coastal towns still in their hands almost without a fight, and knights and burghers embarked for Cyprus. After 191 years, Frankish sovereignty had been finally destroyed.

The Frankish towns and castles suffered a mixed fate. Some depopulated towns and a number of castles which held no strategic value for their new masters were destroyed so as to deprive the Franks of potential bases for use during their repeated raids from Cyprus. Many of the inland strongholds were simply abandoned and gradually fell into decay, but most of the larger ones were not only occupied by the Mamelukes even before the fall of Acre but rebuilt or actually extended (e.g., Margat and Krak). Almost all of them remained seats of local government or straightforward military bases until the end of Mameluke sovereignty in Palestine and Syria. Not until after the Turkish conquest, when the danger of external attack had receded, could the inhabitants of these often remote and badly dilapidated fortresses leave them and move to more comfortable quarters – a fact which explains the comparatively well preserved state of many ruined castles which might otherwise have been used as convenient sources of material for new buildings.

THE KINGDOM OF LESSER ARMENIA 1198-1375

Although Frankish sovereignty in the Levant ended with the fall of Acre, a small Christian bridgehead still existed on the mainland, north of the former Frankish territories. Founded at about the same time as the Frankish states and destined to survive them by only a few decades, the Kingdom of Lesser Armenia was situated in the south-east corner of Asia Minor. It not only represented a major factor in the complex history of the medieval Near East but played an important role as a purveyor of Byzantine and Late Classical cultural and artistic tradition – not least in the field of military architecture.

Originally resident in the mountainous north-east corner of Asia Minor, the Armenians enjoyed centuries of independence under the Bagratid princes, a native dynasty, until the Byzantines reasserted control over them at the beginning of the 11th century. In 1071, after the crushing defeat of Emperor Romanus IV Diogenes at Mantzikert, they were overrun by the Seljuks who were then pouring into Asia Minor. One or two Armenian princes fled southwards and settled in Cilicia, which still belonged to the Byzantine Empire. Here amid the spurs of the Taurus mountains and, later, too, in the fertile plain between Tarsus and Anavarza and the coastal region near Seleucia, there came into being, during the latter half of the 12th century, a small autonomous state composed of numerous formerly independent baronies. The growth of this state, bordered in the north by the wild and inaccessible Taurus and in the east by the Amanus, was attended by alternating disputes with Byzantium and the Principality of Antioch and a series of struggles with the Seljuks who lived in the north. Although nearly destroyed by Emperor John II Comnenus of Byzantium in 1137, the little country soon recovered under the energetic leadership of Thoros II. Thanks to the shrewd diplomacy of its rulers and despite dire threats from the Byzantines in the west, Seljuks in the north and, occasionally, princes of Antioch in the east, the country prospered to such an extent that in 1198 the Armenian prince Leo II requested and was granted royal status by Emperor Henry VI. In spite of incessant disputes between rival Armenian families – disputes in which Frankish factions often became involved because of the close ties of kinship existing between Armenian noblemen and the Frankish nobility of Northern Syria – the little kingdom successfully held its own against all external foes in an unending succession of campaigns. True, the powerful Seljuk sultans of Konya continued to represent a threat until about the middle of the 13th century, but they were deterred from invading Armenian territory too frequently, first, because their attentions were mainly focussed on Byzantium,

and secondly, because the highlands of the Taurus were impassable and guarded by fortifications.

The exiguous remains of the Principality of Antioch continued to act as a buffer between
the Armenians and their powerful Syrian neighbours in the east until 1268, and it was not
until the battle of Darbsac (Trapesac) in 1266, shortly before the fall of Antioch itself, that
they first tasted the mettle of the Egyptian Mameluke armies which were to harass their
little country for almost a century to come. Nevertheless, the far-sighted policies of the
Armenian kings, coupled with assistance from the Mongols and the Western Powers,
managed to defer the inevitable collapse of their sovereignty until the end of the 14th century.
The downfall of the Frankish states left Armenia the only Christian power on the Levantine
mainland. Being closely linked by marriage to the Frankish royal family of Cyprus and, from
1342 onwards, ruled by kings of Lusignan stock, it received aid from the Pope and all the
European countries which were still interested in pursuing the Crusades. Foremost among the
latter were the two great Italian naval powers, Genoa and Venice; these maintained good
commercial relations with Armenia and were only too eager to continue and expand their
trade with the Near East, some of which passed through Armenian ports.

Unlike the Frankish states, which had been based on a rigidly integrated system of feudal
dependence from the outset, the Kingdom of Lesser Armenia had evolved from the host
of small and initially autonomous baronies that had once dotted the country-side between
the Taurus and the Euphrates, each with a fortified town or castle as the nucleus of its
territorial domains. Although the bulk of the towns still retained fortifications dating from
the Byzantine period and some of the castles were modernized Byzantine frontier forts, others
were newly constructed by their Armenian masters. The latter could draw upon an admirable
centuries-old architectural tradition which had produced magnificent examples of ecclesiastical
and secular architecture, not only in the Armenians' original home between Lake Van and
the Caucasus but also in Western Europe and Egypt. Armenian builders and craftsmen had
won a fine reputation in the Byzantine Empire, and it was they who first helped their
inexperienced Frankish neighbours in Syria to improve existing town defences and erect
new castles. It has so far proved impossible to establish beyond doubt whether Frankish
military architecture was still subject to Armenian influence in the 12th and 13th centuries,
but it is not improbable, because contemporary records mention that Armenians were
employed as military engineers by Frankish princes as late as the middle of the 13th century.

Armenian chronicles of later date allude to the existence of a vast number of castles. At
Leo II's coronation festivities, for instance, the attendance list comprised the names of more
than two hundred noblemen who owned castles of their own – and this at a time when the
territory east of the Amanus, nearly all of which originally belonged to Armenian seigneurs,
was already in Muslim hands and had been so since the fall of the County of Edessa. Very
few of these sites have so far been identified and studied, mainly because of their remote
position. The castles, most of which are fairly small, were sited in the rugged and inaccessible
passes and valleys of the Taurus, Anti-Taurus and Amanus ranges. Expatriate Armenian

CAESAREA

noblemen may often have selected these remote sites because they reminded them of their old home in the north, but their chief motive was a wish for security. Thus, the isolation of these castles was dictated by the country's early history, and it engendered a process of architectural development which was entirely independent of, and clearly distinguishable from, Frankish fortification. Favoured sites were isolated rocky knolls and long, inaccessible ridges affording excellent natural protection but very little ground area. Consequently, the shape of Armenian castles was as irregular as the topography to which they had to conform, and the rocky and precipitous terrain in which most of them were situated left so little usable space in the interior that the requisite magazines and offices had to be built in multi-storeyed tiers on the steep slopes. Thus, compared to their Frankish counterparts, which tend to be relatively spacious, Armenian castles have a compact and vertical silhouette which looks more impressive to the modern eye (*cf.* Yılan Kalesi, Sis, and Bağras).

The castles of Lesser Armenia also differ from contemporary Frankish and Arab defensive complexes in numerous details of fortification. While the structure of curtain-walls is similar, discounting frequent variations in stone-mason's technique and fineness of finish imposed by local materials, there is a distinct difference in the shape and disposition of towers. In contrast to the generally rectangular towers and bastions of Frankish and Arab castles, Armenian builders (possibly influenced by Byzantine tradition) favoured semicircular towers, most of which projected a fair distance so as to enfilade the long curtain-walls and protect exposed points. The strong donjon or keep, a widespread feature of Frankish fortification, is rarely found in Armenian castles. In general, despite King Leo II's predilection for the Frankish code of chivalry and way of life, the Franks exerted no perceptible influence on Armenian military architecture. Not until the later years of the kingdom, when it was ruled by Lusignan kings, did fortresses such as Anamur and (in parts) Corycus display details of architectural development which undoubtedly derived from foreign, that is to say, Frankish and Italian, influence.

THE LATIN EMPIRE OF CONSTANTINOPLE AND THE FRANKISH DOMAINS OF MOREA   1204–1460

Barely a year after Armenia's promotion to the status of an independent kingdom had been confirmed by Pope Celestine III, his successor, Innocent III, summoned Western Europe to mount yet another Crusade. In 1202, an army consisting of Italians, Frenchmen and a few Germans embarked at Venice under the command of Boniface, Marquess of Montferrat. After various preliminary skirmishes, it defied the Pope's wishes by attacking Constantinople. The hostility that had grown up between Western Europe and Byzantium since the Second Crusade, coupled with Venetian commercial and political aspirations and the chagrin and exasperation to which the Franks had been condemned by their participation in the dispute over the Byzantine succession, led in 1204 to the imperial city's capture by the Frankish army. In May of that year, after a barbaric orgy of looting, Count Baldwin of Flanders was acclaimed Emperor. Thrace, Macedonia, Salonica, large areas of Greece and parts of Western Asia Minor were swiftly occupied by various sections of the army, and Frankish principalities and fiefs were set up everywhere. On the Byzantine side, Theodore Lascaris of Nicaea endeavoured to unite the Empire's disrupted possessions in Asia Minor, while the Despot Michael mustered Greek forces for a counter-attack from Epirus. After his half-brother and successor, Theodore Angelus, had defeated the Frankish kingdom of Salonica by a surprise assault on its capital and reconquered Thessaly and Macedonia from the Latins, he marched on Constantinople. Outside Adrianople (Edirne), however, he became involved in a protracted dispute with the Emperor of Nicaea, John III Vatatzes. Thanks to internal Greek dissension and the continued assistance of Venice, the Latin Empire, which was now reduced to a small area of Thrace, was able to preserve its tenuous existence for some years more, until, in 1261, Emperor Michael VIII Palaeologus recaptured the ancient capital with Genoese support.

The Frankish domains that had been established in Central and Southern Greece after the great conquest of 1205 proved more durable. The early collapse of the Kingdom of Salonica did not affect the County of Bodonitsa in Central Greece, nor the Duchy of Athens, nor the Peloponnesian principality of Morea, which was made up of twelve separate baronies. During the 13th century, these areas enjoyed a time of peace and prosperity, mainly under the rule of French families. Most of the old Byzantine fortresses (Acrocorinthus, Argos, Calamata, Nauplia, Arcadia and Patras) were rebuilt by their new masters. Some entirely new castles were also constructed (Castel Tornese/Chlemutzi, Mistra, Maina, Karytaina, Navarino and Passava), but the most important of them had to be ceded to the Byzantines in 1262 as ransom for the Prince of Morea, Guillaume de Villehardouin. In 1268, after years of fighting, Byzantine infiltration into a region that had belonged wholly to the Franks since 1205 prompted Guillaume to place Morea under the protection of the powerful house of Anjou, which ruled Sicily and Southern Italy. Athens, Bodonitsa and Euboea preserved their independence, but Athens fell into the hands of a band of Catalan adventurers when the Frankish knights were bloodily defeated at Lake Kopais in 1311. After barely a century, therefore, French noblemen had everywhere been replaced by new seigneurs of the most varied origin. Venice, too, had secured several important footholds in the country, as well as a string of excellently situated harbours (Euboea, Argos and Nauplia, Navarino, Korone and Methone) and large areas of the Aegean archipelago. Although the mutually hostile Italian and Spanish barons of Morea were gradually ousted from the country from 1320 onwards by the Greek despots of Mistra, and Catalan Athens passed in 1387 to the Acciaiuoli, a Florentine family, Greek and Italian sovereignty was ultimately terminated by the ruthless Ottoman conquerors who by 1460 had occupied the whole of Greece with the exception of scattered Venetian bases on the mainland and in the Aegean.

Almost as diverse as the complex family trees of the Frankish families of Morea are the architectural relics of these troubled centuries. The older castles, most of them now in ruins, are a mixture of Byzantine foundations and Frankish additions; the new castles built by the Frankish invaders were reconstructed by the Byzantine despots of Mistra; many of the larger coastal fortresses did not acquire their present appearance until renovated by Venetian military engineers in the 17th century; and, finally, much rebuilding was carried out under Turkish rule. In short, the neat typological development of military architecture exemplified by Crusader buildings in Syria and Palestine has no equivalent in Greece.

The castles of the Frankish period proper, i.e., those dating from between 1205 and the end of the 13th century, were straightforward seats of seignorial authority whose main function was to provide strategically important points from which to control the subjugated country and its alien inhabitants. Discounting local differences in detail and building techniques, they generally conformed to the mountainous terrain and were divided into an upper and a lower fortress. The well-protected core of the defensive system was often dominated by a strong donjon, as at Mistra, while at Castel Tornese (Chlemutzi) the castle itself was designed as a large polygonal donjon with a small open bailey in the interior, like many early Western European castles. The simple donjon is seldom found (as at Pendeskuphi, near Corinth). In Greece, unlike the countries of the Near East, where besiegers always expended vast quantities of man-power and material, armies were weak and insufficiently well-equipped for siege warfare from the very first. Consequently, there was no need for any defensive refinement or over-lavish use of masonry. The castles of Morea seem, in general, to have been totally uninfluenced by the military architecture of Palestine – not unsurprisingly, since the main sponsors of its development there during the latter years of Frankish sovereignty were the great knightly orders, which scarcely put in an appearance on the Greek mainland or in Cyprus, preferring to pursue their traditions in Rhodes and their other possessions in the Eastern Aegean.

THE KINGDOM OF CYPRUS 1192-1473

When the Franks were forced to abandon the few remaining strongholds in their possession after the fall of Acre in 1291 and flee to Cyprus by ship, that prosperous island had already been in Frankish hands for a full century. In 1191, only a few months after his fleet had been compelled to take shelter there by a storm, Richard Cœur de Lion wrested the island from its Byzantine governor and sold it for 100,000 ducats to the Templars, who returned it to him when the local Greeks rose in revolt. In 1192, Richard gave Cyprus to Guy of Lusignan as compensation for losing the throne of Jerusalem, and in 1195 Emperor Henry VI awarded the hereditary monarchy to his brother and successor Amalric of Lusignan. Like

MISTRA

Palestine, Cyprus became embroiled in the disastrous civil war between the Ghibellines and Guelphs after Emperor Frederick II's Crusade in 1229. For many years after the fall of Acre, it constituted the major Christian base in the Eastern Mediterranean and served as a spring-board for Crusade-like expeditions and attacks on the coasts of Anatolia, Syria and Egypt (capture of Alexandria, 1365). The island attained its prime under the energetic leadership of King Peter I (1359-69), but its heyday ended abruptly when he was murdered by disaffected Cypriot noblemen. In 1373 the Genoese seized the opportunity to occupy Famagusta, the island's principal harbour, under the shabbiest of pretexts, and were not dislodged until 1464, after long years of fighting. The power of the kings waned perceptibly – bands of Egyptian Mamelukes ravaged the entire island in 1425 and 1426, virtually unopposed – and finally collapsed in 1473 with the death of the island's last monarch, James II. In 1488, after the brief regency of Caterina Cornaro, the widowed queen, sovereignty passed to the Venetians, who developed the island into a strong outpost of their colonial empire.

The first Turkish invasion of Cyprus in 1527 was repelled, but in 1570 the island swiftly succumbed to a second attack made in greater strength. The fortress of Nicosia, which had been undergoing reconstruction for some years, fell after a seven-week siege, whereas the harbour of Famagusta, which Venetian military engineers had reinforced with strong towers and bastions as early as 1492, resisted the Turks for almost a year.

The other fortifications on the island which had been improved under Venetian rule – the forts at Kyrenia and Paphos – played no part in these battles. As for the island's few medieval castles, these had already been dismantled c. 1525 because they no longer fulfilled the require-ments of contemporary warfare. Instead of spending money on these old defence works, the Venetians had decided to modernize the major fortified harbours and re-design the bastioned defences of the capital, Nicosia, on a grand scale.

Unlike the Holy Land, where the building of fortifications became an ineluctable necessity because of the continual risk of attack (and was certainly not undertaken from motives of architectural self-indulgence), Cyprus seldom found itself threatened by external foes. The building of fortifications was a royal prerogative there, with the result that, apart from a few largish castles erected by the crown, the only fortified buildings were produced by the knightly orders. Rocky eyries such as Kantara, Buffavento and St Hilarion (Dieudamour), perched on crags or nestling against the steep slopes of the northern coastal range, are strongly reminiscent of Armenian castles, not only by reason of their unique sites but because they possess many of the same features (semicircular flanking towers, courtyards, etc.). Apart from these, other isolated donjon-type strongholds existed in the plain (Kolossi, possibly Limassol), as well as small forts with corner-towers (Siguri, possibly Gastria). Romantic though they look today, none of these castles played any part in the subsequent development of military architecture because of the progress already made by the art of fortification in Palestine during the 13th century. Not until the turn of the 15th-16th centuries, when the island was menaced by Turkish invasion, did Cyprus come to share the lead in the develop-ment of modern systems of fortification with Rhodes. Venetian military architects, who had been in a position to observe a surprisingly rapid metamorphosis in the art of fortification in cities adjacent to the Venetian Terra Ferma (Ferrara, Padua, Crema, Verona, Milan, etc.) during the wars between Emperor Charles V and King Francis I of France, now designed and built fortresses in the new style in Cyprus. What was more, the power and wealth of the Signoria enabled them to draw up designs on a grand scale, such as the plan for renovating the defences of Nicosia. Though never completed, this strictly proportioned bastionary defensive system might have been taken from a contemporary text-book on the theory of fortification.

HOSPITALLERS IN THE AEGEAN 1306-1522

For many of the Franks who had fled from Palestine, Cyprus became a new home where they could live a freer, more peaceful life, untrammelled by constant fears of Muslim attack. This new-found peace satisfied everyone but the military knights who had also fled to Cyprus and to whom the rich island offered few prospects of employment. Whilst the Templars had retired to France, only to be brutally suppressed in 1312, the Hospitallers, after a brief sojourn in Cyprus during the years 1291-1310, established a new autonomous domain in the Eastern Aegean. Between 1306 and 1309, operating from the mainland of Asia Minor, which was in process of occupation by the Seljuks, they conquered the island of Rhodes, nominally a possession of the Byzantine Emperor but one whose favourable position between the Aegean and Eastern Mediterranean made it an ideal base for the Hospitallers' future operations. From Rhodes, they extended their sphere of authority to the southern Sporades and joined the Cypriot fleet in a series of large-scale raids on the Syrian and Egyptian coasts during the 14th century. In 1374 they acquired Smyrna (Izmir) on the west coast of Asia Minor, which had been captured by a league of Christian powers, but their attempt to gain a foothold on the Greek mainland in 1400 was frustrated by the resistance of the native population.

The loss of Smyrna in 1415 heralded a century-long struggle with the Ottoman Turks. The Hospitallers succeeded in developing the small port of Halicarnassus, situated opposite their stronghold on Cos, into a mainland base which could serve as a substitute for the important harbour of Smyrna, but firm limits were imposed on further expansion by the menacing attitude of the Turks, who attacked Rhodes and Cos in strength as early as 1455. By 1470, the Hospitallers (like the Venetians in Cyprus a few years later) had been compelled to forgo the improvement of all their numerous castles and concentrate on adapting their principal bases (Rhodes itself, Cos, and the new castle of St Peter at Halicarnassus) to modern requirements. Stout walls and a resolute defence enabled the Hospitallers to repel the Ottomans' second large-scale assault and raise the siege of Rhodes in 1480, but this success only encouraged them to pursue the improvement of their main fortifications with greater zeal. By 1520, thanks to the energetic leadership of Grand Master Pierre d'Aubusson (1476–1503), the Hospitallers had turned Rhodes into what was probably the strongest and most up-to-date fortress in the Western world. In December 1522, however, when stocks of ammunition were at an end and all hope of relief had vanished, the city was forced to surrender to the Turks after holding out for the better part of a year. The Hospitallers evacuated all their Aegean possessions, withdrew to Italy, and were granted a new base on the island of Malta by Emperor Charles V.

The fortification of Rhodes and the strongholds of Cos and St Peter during the 15th–16th centuries represented a renaissance in the Aegean archipelago of the great old architectural tradition which the Hospitallers had founded in the Holy Land when they built the castles of Krak and Margat. True, the beginnings of this process were modest, and few large-scale examples of military architecture came into being at first. The 14th century witnessed the construction of the relatively simple defences of the Hospital and the town of Rhodes itself, while small castles already in existence on captured islands were gradually renovated on a modest scale. In the absence of acute danger, the Hospitallers were able to emulate the Frankish overlords of Greece, and of Cyprus until the mid-15th century, by limiting themselves to fortifications of an unpretentious nature. Like the central core of St Peter's, most of these presented a wholly medieval appearance, although isolated innovations did occur, as, for instance, in Rhodes, where there was a consistent use of free-standing towers which were only loosely linked to the main line of defence.

It is, of course, difficult to compare fortifications built in the first half of the 15th century with castles built in Syria almost two centuries earlier. In Europe, cannon were first used against medieval castles about half-way through the 14th century, and a century later the new weapon had been developed to such an extent that it was no longer an occasional begetter of local successes but a universally respected instrument of war. The impression made by heavy cannon on the massive walls of the ancient imperial city of Constantinople in 1453 had early convinced the Turks of the potentialities of the new weapon and prompted them to substitute modern ordnance for medieval siege-engines and techniques. Now that these new offensive weapons were in the hands of their principal foe, the knights of Rhodes were forced to devise new defensive installations. They did not, however, embark on the systematic improvement of the obsolete defences of Rhodes (with the aid of Italian engineers) until persuaded to do so by bitter experience gained in the siege of 1480 – almost at the same time as the Venetians began to renovate the town fortifications of Famagusta.

Since enemy attacks were still directed primarily against curtain-walls, even in the era of the cannon, the first step was to reinforce the interior of old walls with deep banks of earth (ramparts) which would resist bombardment and provide scope for the deployment of the defenders' own cannon. At Rhodes, the walls were increased in thickness from nearly 7 feet to 17 feet in 1481, and again in 1521 to a total depth of 37 feet. The ditches were widened at the same time and, in places, doubled, and broad terrepleins were installed in front of the new barbicans, most of which were polygonal. Towers received special attention. During the 13th century, medieval exponents of fortification were still concentrating on the defence of vulnerable curtain-walls. It was only in the course of this century that they recognized – and, in new fortifications, exploited – the opportunity to enfilade curtain-walls from towers (as in the outer ring of defences at Krak or in Armenian castles). By a process of logical transition, the main instruments of defence, i. e., cannon, were now mounted where they could exert the strongest enfilading effect on attackers, that is to say, in towers reinforced for this purpose. At Rhodes, the old small rectangular towers were enclosed by massively constructed outworks of polygonal or semicircular design in which the guns were mounted on open platforms or in vaulted casemates. Rhodes possessed the first-known polygonal bastions, born of improvisation in 1521. Although semicircular bastions (rondels) and rondel-like constructions were still in the majority both there and in the fortresses of St Peter and Cos, practical experience and a theoretical knowledge of the mathematical principles of ballistics soon combined to influence development in favour of the polygonal bastion. We know this because only six years later, in 1527, Michele Sanmicheli built a polygonal bastion (the Bastione delle Maddalene) in Verona in place of the earlier rondel, and because these bastions quickly became the main feature of a complete defensive system known as the 'Old Italian', which spread from the Mediterranean area to the whole of Europe in the course of the 16th century and became the basis of all modern fortification.

Several minor expeditions against the Turkish-held western coast of Asia Minor were recognized as Crusades by the Church as late as the first half of the 14th century, and in the middle of the same century King Peter I of Cyprus was still making serious attempts to mount a general Crusade with the object of recapturing Jerusalem. Before many years had passed, however, the West had to renounce further expeditions to the Levant because its own frontiers were in jeopardy. The Ottoman Turks had destroyed the Kingdom of Serbia by their victory at Kosovo ('The Field of Blackbirds') in 1389 and were now threatening to march on Hungary. In 1395-6, at the instigation of King Sigismund of Hungary, almost all the great European powers contributed to the mounting of a large Crusader army which was to drive back the Turks and, if possible, wipe them out. It had scarcely set foot on Turkish territory, however, before Sultan Bâyezid I completely annihilated it in a fierce battle at Nicopolis. The Crusaders had at least compelled the Sultan to raise the siege of Constantinople, and he never resumed it. In 1402, after his army had sustained a severe defeat at Angora (Ankara), Bâyezid was taken prisoner by Timur, the Mongol ruler.

The imperial city ultimately fell to Bâyezid's grandson, Mehmet II Fatih. A few years later, in 1464, Pope Pius II died just as he was about to embark, alone and unsupported by any Western monarch, on the Crusade which he had preached so indefatigably. After four centuries, the era of the Crusades had finally come to an end.

FOREWORD

My purpose in compiling this catalogue was to provide a brief review – divorced from any wider historical examination – of the structural components and history of each fortress, together with all the major factors which affected its construction. The following plans and particulars should enable every reader to check structural relationships and suggested datings for himself, thus forming an independent picture of his own. In view of the large number of buildings involved and wide variations in the quality of research carried out hitherto, shortage of space has presented numerous problems of the type which beset any summary.

Lengthy descriptions of sites and methods of construction have been avoided because many details can be deduced from the plans and others from the notes on the plates. The plans were specially redrawn for the present work, and an attempt was made to adhere to a common scale where possible, though the widely varying sizes of individual fortresses and the relative inaccuracy of many existing plans has necessitated the use of different scales (mostly 1:1000 and 1:2000). Town and site plans are also given where necessary. Information about individual castles has been limited to particulars which have a bearing on their architectural history; data of purely genealogical or military interest have been omitted. I have been compelled not only to rely heavily on existing literature but, in some cases, to accept debatable points without further discussion, since lack of space has made it impossible to identify sources or explore individual problems. No source-references are supplied in the bibliographies appended to the notes on each castle — merely the titles of major publications, most of which are sufficiently specific about their sources. Apart from the monographic treatises quoted (the titles of which have frequently been omitted altogether), numerous particulars have been taken from the major historical works of Cl. Cahen, R. Grousset and Sir Steven Runciman, to whose indices reference should be made in every instance.

Certain inconsistencies arose over the transliteration of proper names and the present-day names of many castles, for which the contemporary local designation and spelling have been used wherever possible. With a few added simplifications designed to enhance the readability of the text, the transliteration of Arab names conforms to the rules laid down by H. Wehr in his *Arabisches Wörterbuch für die Schriftsprache der Gegenwart.* The small table below indicates the pronunciation of individual letters as they occur in Turkish and Arab names:

Turkish	Arabic	English equivalent
c	ǧ	j as in jam
ç		ch as in champion
ğ		usually omitted
h	ḥ	strongly aspirated h
ı		short i as in pencil
j		s as in pleasure
k	q	k
s	ṣ	strongly sibilated s
ş	š	sh as in sham

Here, as in the Introduction, the original French spelling of old names has often been retained where it is in current literary use.

TRIPOLI

Plates 9–11

Gr. Tripolis; Frk. Triple, etc.; the castle settlement: Mont Pèlerin, Mons Pelerinus, Mons Peregrinus, Arab. Tarablûs; the castle itself: Qal 'at Sanğîl.

Description

Town and port on the northern coast of Lebanon, occupying the site of an ancient settlement and for centuries an important harbour serving Damascus.

The town now consists of two parts: the port of al-Mina, which stands on the site of the ancient and medieval settlement, a small peninsula with a harbour well protected by reefs; and the modern residential quarter on the mountainous slopes above, grouped round the medieval castle and straddling the Nahr Qadîša (also Nahr Abû 'Alî). Founded only after the Arab reconquest of 1289, the town was not heavily fortified but relied for its protection on the castle which stands on a rocky ridge above it. Of the castle, very few relics of the Frankish era survive, the bulk of it having been newly constructed under Arab and Turkish rule.

The harbour settlement – the residential quarter proper until 1289 – was guarded on the seaward side by six strong towers dating from the 14th–15th centuries. No remnants of the original town defences survive, but according to early travellers' accounts the entire peninsula was protected by a cross-wall complete with towers and ditches.

History

1099. Under Fatimid rule until acquired by the Banû 'Ammâr in 1070, the town is attacked by Frankish Crusaders on their way to Jerusalem but manages to purchase its freedom.

1102–3. After the conquest of Tartûs, Count Raymond de St. Gilles lays siege to Tripoli, which promptly forms an alliance with the Atâbeg of Damascus and continues to receive reinforcements by sea despite the intervention of a small Genoese fleet. For added protection, the besiegers erect a fort on the Mons Pelerinus, near the town.

1105–9. The siege continues after Raymond's death, but the town is not compelled to surrender until attacked in greater strength by his son Bertrand. Tripoli then becomes the seat of the Counts of Tripoli and remains so until their line dies out.

1157 and 1170. Earthquakes cause widespread damage in the town and its immediate vicinity.

1187. On the death of the last count, Raymond III, the Toulouse dynasty becomes extinct and Tripoli passes to the Principality of Antioch.

1244. Khwarezmian mercenaries raid the town, looting it and inflicting severe damage.

1266. An Arab army under Sultan Baibars invades the region and captures numerous block-forts on the road to Tripoli. In subsequent years, Tripoli becomes a focus of inter-Frankish disputes between Bohemond VII of Antioch and Guy II of Giblet. Military knights and citizens are also involved in these conflicts, which cause havoc in the town.

1289. The army of Sulton Qala'ûn captures Tripoli after barely two months' siege. The Genoese and Venetian burghers flee by ship shortly before.

The entire Frankish harbour town is destroyed to deter possible Frankish landings from Cyprus, and a new residential quarter is built at the foot of the castle.

1307–9. Improvement of the castle by the Arab governor, Saif ad-dîn Esendemir Kurğî. New building work carried out in the town.

Tripoli remained the seat of the provincial governor and, thus, one of the most important towns in Syria until outstripped by Beirut in the 19th century.

Bibliography:
Enc. Isl. IV, 714–5 (Fr. Buhl 1934);
v. Berchem-Fatio, *Voyage I,* 116–122;
v. Berchem – M. Sobernheim, *Matériaux pour un Corpus Inscr. Arabicarum,* Vol. II, 1 *(Syrie du Nord),* Cairo 1909, 37–139 (MIFAO 25);
J. Richard, *Le Comté de Tripoli sous la Dynastie Toulousaine (1102–1187),* Paris 1945, pass.

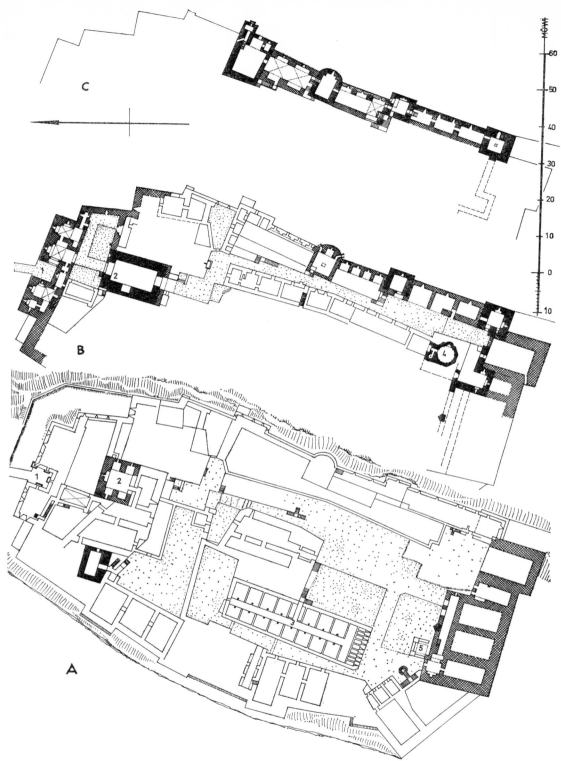

Plan 1: TRIPOLI – MONS PEREGRINUS. *Ground-plans of the castle, scale 1:1000. A, Plan of present ground-level. B, Plan of first sub-level. C, Plan of second sub-level. Frankish portions in black, early Arab additions and alterations cross-hatched, later Arab additions hatched, Turkish additions unshaded. 1, Gatehouse. 2, Donjon. 3, Stable-block. 4, Frankish chapel (newly excavated). 5, Islamic burial-place. (Based on author's surveys.)*

44

SAHYUN

Plates 12–21

Gr. Sigon; Frk. Saone, Sahaune, etc.; Arab. Ṣahyûn Ṣihyaun.

Description

Ruined castle situated on an elongated ridge between two deep gorges in the Nuṣairî Mountains,
roughly fifteen miles north-east of the sea-port of
Lattaqia as the crow flies. The fortifications cover an
area of some 12½ acres, and are separated from the
rest of the plateau to the north by a rock-hewn fosse
about 160 yards long, 60 feet wide and 90 feet deep.
The castle, which sprawls along the ridge in a series
of separate terraces running from north-east to
south-west, is over 760 yards long and between 55
and 160 yards wide. The rocky slopes flanking it
fall away steeply to the two river-valleys below.

The Middle Byzantine nucleus of the castle, part
of which was built over by the Franks, is badly
dilapidated, and very little of it has yet been unearthed. It consists of double walls situated a short
distance apart, some semicircular towers, and an
inner citadel.

Frankish builders of the 12th century concentrated on strengthening the main north-east face abutting on the plateau. Apart from the almost insur-
mountable fosse, they built the large donjon and
adjoining walls, which were reinforced with semicircular bastions. While the long north face enjoyed the natural protection of rocky precipices,
the more accessible south face had to be secured by
a stout wall set with massive rectangular towers.
The heavily fortified upper bailey was cut off from
the more rambling lower bailey by a cross-wall
which skilfully exploited a natural ravine. Communication between the upper and lower baileys was
via two posterns, one large and one small, the lower
fortress having two gates of its own, one on either
flank. The simple perimeter walls of the lower bailey, which extend far to the south-west, cling closely
to the rocky terrain and are reinforced only by
small bastions at a few points.

The architectural remains in the interior of the
upper fortress date partly from the Byzantine period
(the old cross-walls have largely survived) and
partly from the Frankish period, but mostly from
the long era of Arab occupation (mosque and baths).
The ruins of a small village can be discerned just
outside the castle on the long ridge of high ground
to the north-east.

Ṣahyûn, which was abandoned in the late Middle
Ages, exemplifies more clearly than most other Sy-

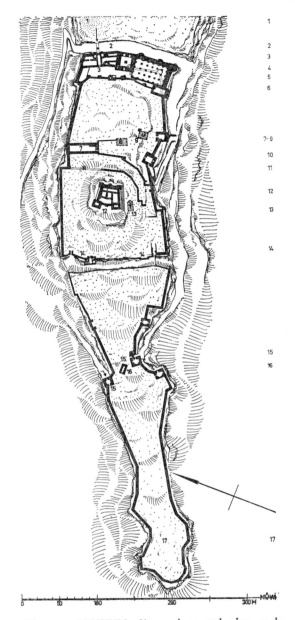

Plan 2: SAHYUN. *Site and general plan, scale
1:5000. 1, Remains of medieval village. 2, Fosse.
3, Main gate and (first) Byzantine cross-wall. 4,
Large magazine constructed above latter. 5 and 6,
Remains of second Byzantine cross-wall. 7, Cistern.
8 and 9, Baths and mosque, both dating from the
Arab period. 10 and 11, Second and third Byzantine cross-walls. 12, Byzantine inner citadel. 13,
Small Frankish chapel. 14, South-west cross-wall
and fosse. 15, Gates of lower fortress. 16, Chapel.
17, Lower bailey. (Based on Deschamps, Châteaux
I, 80, and author's surveys).*

rian castles the forms of fortification current in the early and mid-12th century.

History

c. 975. Emperor John I Tzimisces of Byzantium (969–976) captures the site from the Hamdanids of Aleppo while campaigning in Northern Syria. Fortifications, citadel and probably the two outer wall systems are presumed to have been built thereafter.

Early 12th century. Captured by the Franks at some indeterminate date, perhaps after the conquest of Lattaqia in 1108. A Count Robert de Sahyoun ('Le Lépreux') is mentioned in 1119.

1188. Saladin besieges the castle in the course of his victorious campaign and captures it after intensive bombardment with mangonels because the perimeter proves too large for its small garrison to defend.

1188–1272. Ṣahyûn passes into the possession of Emir Nâṣir ad-dîn Manguwiriš and remains a family fief until 1272, when his heirs are forced to cede the castle to Sultan Baibars of Egypt.

A mosque is built inside the castle under Sultan Qala'ûn. Sahyûn subsequently plays a brief role in the history of Northern Syria, but is abandoned in the course of the Middle Ages and falls into decay.

1840. The Turkish-held castle is bombarded by the army of Ibrahim Pasha, sustaining severe damage.

Bibliography:
Enc. Isl. IV, 447 (P. Schwarz 1934);
v. Berchem – Fatio, *Voyage I*, 267–283, and *II*, Pl. 59–62; P. Deschamps, 'Le château de Saône dans la Principauté d'Antioche', in: *Gazette des Beaux-Arts*, Dec. 1930, 329–364;
P. Deschamps, 'Le château de Saône et ses premiers seigneurs', in: *Syria 16*, 1935, 73–88;
R. Fedden, *Crusader Castles*, London 1950, 46–50;
Fedden – Thomson, 72–76.

QAL'AT SUBEIBE   *Plate 22*

Frk. often Belinas, Paneas, etc., after name of nearby town; Arab. Qal 'at Nemrûd, name of town: Bâniyâs.

Description

Castle in the southern spurs of the Anti-Lebanon (ancient designation Hermon, modern ǧebel aš-Šaiḥ), situated immediately to the north of the small town of Bâniyâs in the Syro-Israeli border country, near the sources of the Jordan. It occupies a long ridge overlooking a high plateau which rises slightly to the north, and its main defences face the mountains in the north.

The moderate gradient of the southern slope necessitated heavier fortifications on this flank, which was well protected by eight towers and bastions of varying size and design. The northern flank enjoyed the natural protection of a steep rocky slope and was only guarded by a simple wall of polygonal lay-out. The western flank, being less favoured by topographical conditions, was protected, like the southern flank, by several strong towers.

Owing to its position on the Syro-Israeli border, the site has been out of bounds for years.

History

1126. The first stronghold to be acquired by the Persian Ismaelites (later known as the Assassins), Subeibe is evacuated by the sect as a result of religious persecution in Damascus and handed over to the Franks.

1129. King Baldwin II occupies Subeibe and gives it in fee to Renier Brus. The defences of castle and town are improved at this period.

1132. The castle is captured by Tâǧ al-Muluk Bûrî, ruler of Damascus.

1139. As a result of inter-Arab rivalry between the rulers of Damascus and Aleppo, Subeibe is jointly besieged and taken by the Franks and Damascenes. It is restored to its original owners.

1157. After several attempts, Sultan Nûr ad-dîn of Aleppo succeeds in capturing the town of Belinas, but the castle is stubbornly defended by Onfroy II of Toron, Constable of the Kingdom of Jerusalem. The fortifications are repaired after the siege has been raised.

1164. Renewed attack on the castle by Nûr ad-dîn while Onfroy is campaigning in Egypt with

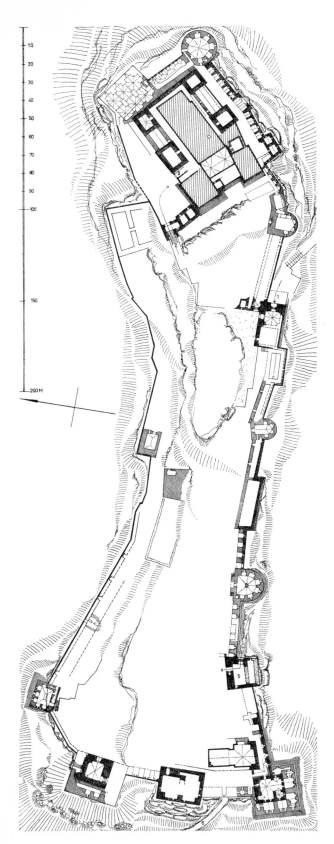

King Amalric. It is forced to surrender after a lengthy siege, and falls into Arab hands.

1174. Investment of the castle by a Frankish army under King Amalric, who dies during the siege. Subeibe remains in Arab possession.

1219. In view of Frankish successes during the Fifth Crusade, the castle is dismantled by al-Mu 'azzam, Emir of Damascus, to prevent the Franks from using it as a base for their threatened attack on Damascus.

1226–30. Restoration of the castle by Othman. Preliminary rebuilding is followed by further work undertaken in 1239, 1260 and, finally, in the reign of Sultan Baibars.

The castle lost its importance after the Middle Ages and gradually fell into decay.

Bibliography:
Enc. Isl. I, 664 (Buhl); *Enc. Isl. (2)I*, 1048, s. v. Bâniyâs; Deschamps, *Châteaux II*, 145–174, containing full bibliographical data;
M. van Berchem, *Le Château de Baniâs et ses inscriptions'*, in: *Journ. Asiatique*, 8th Series, Vol. 12, 1888, 466 et seq.

Plan 3: QAL'AT SUBEIBE – PANEAS. *General plan of castle, scale 1:2000. Buildings of the Frankish period (1129–1132) in black, ditto (putative) cross-hatched, Arab constructions (post-1164) closely hatched, horizontal section through soil and rock widely hatched. 1, Main exterior gate. 2, Inner gate to citadel. 3, Gate of citadel proper. 4, Lower fortress. 5, Side gate of lower fortress. 6, Present approach-road. (Based on Deschamps, Châteaux II.)*

AL-KERAK

Plates 23–27

Gr. Charachmoba; Frk.-Lat. Le Crac de Montréal,
Petra deserti, Civitas Petracensis, etc.; Arab. Al-
Kerak.

Description

Town and castle in Southern Jordan, almost ten
miles east of the southern end of the Dead Sea,
situated on a spur of rock whose flanks fall away
steeply to the Wâdî Kerak, which divides into the
Wâdî as-Sitt and Wâdî al-Franǧi just beneath the
fortress. Just south of the town, covering it against
attack from the only neighbouring high ground,
stands the castle itself, built on two terraces and
separated from the town by a deep fosse. The
town was also enclosed by a perimeter wall which
followed the contours of the rocks, but this has been
largely dismantled in recent times.

The extant defences date, in roughly equal proportions, from the Frankish and Arab periods. The
two phases are distinguishable by the stone employed, which came from different quarries.

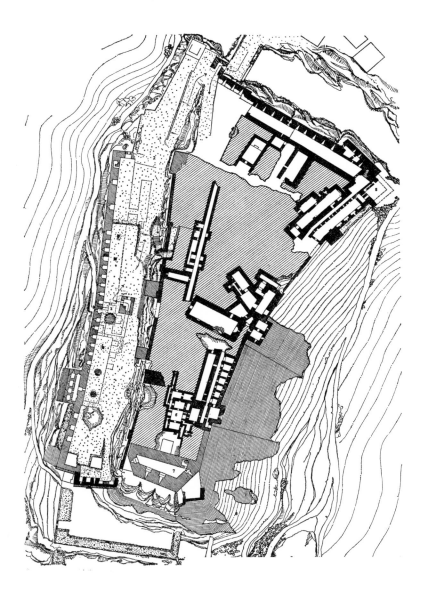

Plan 4: AL-KERAK.
Ground-plan of upper and
lower fortress, scale 1:2000.
The plan shows premises
which lie beneath the
ground-level of the upper
fortress, and the lower
fortress has also been
pierced at ground-level to
reveal subterranean
chambers, which are
indicated by stippling. The
first and second Frankish
structural phases (1142–88)
are black and cross-hatched,
buildings of the Arab
period (post-1188) closely
hatched, and substructures
obscured by soil and rock
widely hatched. 1, Modern
main gate. 2, Lower
fortress. 3, Lower gate.
4, Outer wall of lower
fortress. 5, North-east
corner-tower (destroyed).
6, 'Palace premises.
7, Donjon. 8, Revetment.

History

Early 12th century. Already a place of long-standing importance, Kerak is occupied by the Franks, probably during their early campaigns under King Baldwin I. The town fortifications may also have been improved at this time.

1142. As part of the plan to consolidate Frankish Transjordan, the socal feudal seigneur, Payen le Bouteiller (Paganus Pincerna), decrees the improvement of the town and its defences and the construction of the castle, which is further strengthened under his successors.

1170. The castle is briefly besieged by Nûr addîn of Damascus to safeguard the passage of a caravan bound for Egypt. As an outpost on the main north-south route, Kerak possesses considerable strategic importance. Saladin besieges it again for a short time in 1173.

1177. Castle and fief pass to Reynald of Châtillon, a courageous but imprudent man whose incessant raids provoke Saladin into attacking Frankish territory.

1183–4. First siege of Kerak, interrupted by the approach of King Baldwin IV. A second siege directed by Saladin ends similarly in 1184, after seven weeks.

1187-8. No immediate steps are taken against Kerak after the Franks' defeat at Hattîn in 1187, but the castle is invested in the following year and forced to surrender in November 1188, after a siege of eight months. Saladin bestows the important stronghold on his brother al-Malik al-'Ādil, who repairs and strenghtens its defences. Since the castle is reputed to be impregnable, Saladin uses it as his treasury. After the death of al-'Ādil, the contents of this treasury are inherited by his son, al-Malik al-Mu'azzam.

Early 13th century. Kerak plays an important role in the negotiations for the return of Jerusalem because the Franks believe that they cannot retain possession of the Holy City without it. Despite this, Kerak is confirmed and acknowledged as an Arab possession when Jerusalem is restored to Emperor Frederick II in 1219.

1264. Sultan Baibars strengthens the castle and town defences after capturing Kerak from the last Ayyubid prince. Construction of north bastion of the town wall and improvement of the castle fosse.

1293. An earthquake causes severe damage which it takes until 1309 to make good. During this period, Kerak attains a certain importance as a place of exile, also as a place of retreat used by renegade members of the ruling families.

Although it remained an administrative centre until the end of the Mameluke era, Kerak entirely lost its importance after the Turkish conquest of Syria. Its defences, which were still in a good state of preservation in about 1870, were not dismantled until the close of the 19th century.

Bibliography:
Enc. Isl. II, 905–6 (Fr. Buhl 1927);
P. Deschamps, *Châteaux II*, 35–98, with extensive bibliographical data;
A. Musil, *Arabia Petraea* (Vienna 1907) Vol. I: Moab, 45–62, with plan.

BAĞRAS   Plates 28–31

Gr. Pagrai; Frk. Bagaras or (more freq.) Gastun, Gastin, Guaston, etc.; Turk. Bağras.

Description

Castle and small village in the Hatay, situated among the eastern spurs of a mountain range formed by the Kizil daği and Amanus. Like the block-fort commanding the Beylan Pass itself, this was one of the key-points on the Antioch-Iskenderun-(Alexandretta)-Cilicia route. The castle, which is fairly well preserved, lies some way up a mountain valley on a cone of rock which falls away steeply on all sides. Because of the steepness of the rocky slopes, the castle was built on several levels connected by passages and steps. It thus evolved entirely from the terrain, and its compact design is reminiscent of many Armenian castles in Cilicia. Apart from numerous vaulted chambers and passages built into the slopes, the remains of two large halls have survived in the upper fortress. At the foot of the castle stood a large aqueduct which also served to block the upper part of the valley.

History

1097. Probably constructed by the Byzantines in the 10th century, the castle is occupied by the Crusaders, perhaps during the siege of Antioch.
1108. Bağras is designated an Antiochene possession by the Treaty of Durazzo.

1153. The castle is handed over to the Templars and its defences are presumed to have been improved at this period. It plays an important role in conflicts between the Franks and Armenians, also between local Arab princes.

1188. Siege and capture of the castle by Saladin, who abandons and dismantles it on hearing news of the approach of Emperor Frederick I (Barbarossa).

1191. Forestalling the Antiochenes, the Armenians occupy the place and repair its defences, thereby sowing the seeds of a long-standing dispute between the two parties.

1268. The castle, probably abandoned after the fall of Antioch, is occupied by Sultan Baibars. It retains its importance until the Ottoman occupation of Syria.

Bibliography:
Enc. Isl. I, 593 (R. Hartmann 1913); *Enc. Isl.* (2)I, 937 (Cl. Cahen 1960);
Cl. Cahen, *La Syrie du Nord à l'époque des Croisades,* Paris 1940, pass.;
Guide Bleu: Turquie, Paris 1958, 465.

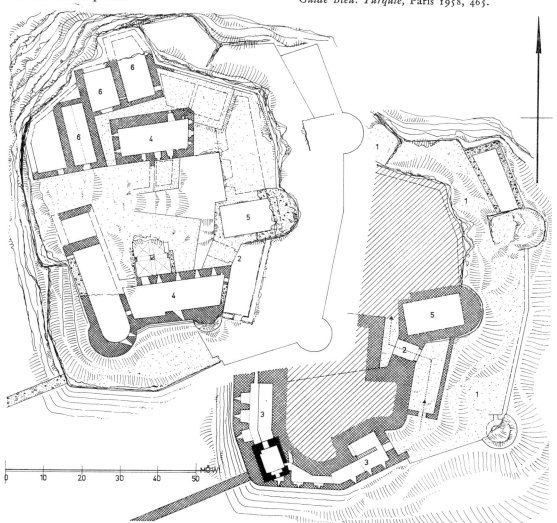

Plan 5: BAĞRAS. *Ground-plans of the castle, scale 1:1000. A, Lower fortress and lower floor of upper fortress. B, Upper floor of upper fortress (ground-floor premises stippled) with the earlier building phase (Byzantine?) in black and the portions dating from the 12th-13th centuries cross-hatched. 1, Lower fortress. 2, Forecourt and gatehouse. 3, Lower gallery. 4, Palace premises. 5, Great Tower. 6, Magazine chambers. (Based on author's survey.)*

AKKAR   Plate 32

Frk. Akkar; Arab. Ḥiṣn ʻAkkâr al-ʻatîqa.

Description

Small ruined castle in North Lebanon (approximately 25 miles north-east of Tripoli) situated on a mountainous ridge on the northern slopes of the ğebel ʻAkkâr. Part of the northern frontier defences of the County, it was in visual communication with Chastel Blanc and Krak des Chevaliers. The asymmetrical site was protected on the side facing the mountains by a strong donjon and a deep fosse. Only isolated remnants of the outer walls survive, among them two towers.

History

1094. Originally a family seat but later held by the Fatimids, the castle comes under Seljuk jurisdiction. In 1109, after the capture of Tripoli, Akkar, too, is captured from the Seljuk atabêgs of Damascus by the Franks.

c. 1160-70 The castle is briefly reoccupied by Nûr ad-dîn of Aleppo, but by 1170 it is again in Frankish hands. King Amalric gives it to the Hospitallers, a bequest which Raymond III of Tripoli may have confirmed after his release from captivity. The castle later passes to the rulers of Nephin (now Enfé).

1271. On 29 May, after being besieged for about a month by the army of Sultan Baibars, Akkar surrenders because the Sultan has succeeded in bringing artillery to bear on the castle. The garrison is permitted to withdraw to Tripoli.

Late 13th century. The castle is restored under Arab rule, and remains in use until destroyed by the Druse Emir Fakhraddîn (1595–1634).

Bibliography:
Dussaud-Deschamps-Seyrig, *La Syrie antique et médiévale...* Paris 1931, 146–7;
M. van Berchem – M. Sobernheim, *Matériaux pour un Corpus Inscr. Arabicarum*, Vol. II, 1 (*Syrie du Nord*), Cairo 1909, 2–14 (MIFAO 25);
Guide Bleu: Moyen Orient, Paris 1956, 110 et seq.

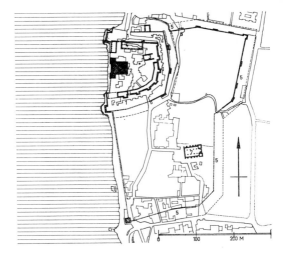

Plan 6: TARTUS. *Town plan, scale 1:10,000. (Dotted lines represent sections of wall which no longer exist.) 1, Forecourt of Templar fortress. 2, Donjon. 3, Ruined chapel. 4, Great Hall (chapterhouse?). 5, Town wall (partially destroyed). 6, Town gate. 7, St Mary's Cathedral. (Based on Deschamps, Châteaux I, 60.)*

TARTUS   Plates 33–35

Frk. Tortosa, Tortouse, etc., after the ancient name Antaradus, Antarsus; Arab. Ṭarṭûs, Anṭarṭûs.

Description

Medieval sea-port and place of pilgrimage occupying the site of a large ancient settlement on the Syrian coast. The small town possessed a simple perimeter wall guarded by towers, and had a strong citadel at its north-west corner. Ditches and outer walls surrounded an inner wall reinforced with rectangular towers. Abutting on the interior were the 'Great Hall' in the north and, distributed round the other sides, simple living-quarters and magazines in the form of long vaulted passages. Immediately beside the sea stood a strong donjon-like tower of which only relics of the foundations still exist.

In the residential quarter stands the recently restored Church of St Mary. Originally built between 1123 and the beginning of the 13th century, it was a cathedral and important pilgrims' church during the Frankish period.

History

1099. Temporarily occupied by the Byzantines during the 10th century, the town is captured by Crusaders on their way to Jerusalem but reoccupied after their withdrawal by the Emir of Tripoli.

1102. Siege and capture of Tartus by Raymond de St Gilles, assisted by a Genoese fleet. Raymond establishes his residence there until the capture of Tripoli.

1152. Brief occupation of the town by Nûr ad-dîn of Aleppo. After its recapture, King Baldwin III gives it to the Templars (c. 1152–8), who establish their main headquarters there and completely reconstruct the harbour and fortifications.

1188. While campaigning in Northern Syria, Saladin captures the town and parts of the Templar fortress, though the knights in one strong tower manage to withstand the Arab assault. Saladin severely damages the town, the church of St Mary, which has been under construction since 1123, and the fortifications. The repair and improvement of defence installations recommences immediately, and work continues on the cathedral.

1267. The town manages to buy off an attack by Sultan Baibars by paying tribute, but is attacked again in 1270.

1291. Tortosa is captured after a brief siege and the knights flee to Cyprus by ship, taking the celebrated image of the Virgin Mary from the cathedral.

1300–2. Knights Templars continue to occupy the off-shore island of Rouâd, but are expelled in 1302 by Sultan Nâsir Muḥammad.

1367–9. Under the command of King Peter I, Cypriot naval units launch abortive attacks on the town and the island of Rouâd.

1518. Another group of Frankish knights settles on Rouâd but is quickly dislodged.

The town played no major role in the late Middle Ages or in modern times. Recently, houses have sprung up among the buildings of the citadel, parts of which still survive.

Bibliography:
Rey, *Arch. Militaire*, 69 et seq., 211 et seq., and Pl. 8;
v. Berchem – Fatio, *Voyage I*, 320–334;
Enlart, *Monuments II*, 395–430;
Enc. Isl. IV, 736–7 (E. Honigmann 1934);
Jean Richard, *Le Comté de Tripoli sous la dynastie Toulousaine (1102–1187)*, Paris 1945, pass.

SAFITA

Plates 36–39

Frk. Chastel Blanc; Arab. Safita, Safitha, Burğ as-Safîtâ, etc.

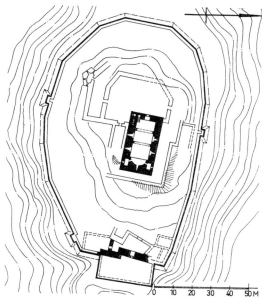

Plan 7: SAFITA – CHASTEL BLANC. *Ground-plan, scale 1:2000, showing condition of castle at about the middle of the 19th century. (Based on Rey, Arch. Militaire, Pl. 9.)*

Description

Small town and castle in the southern coastal region of Syria, lying at just over 1000 feet above sea level and situated on a rocky knoll in the southern spurs of the Nūsairî mountains, a favourable position which ensured visual communication with almost all the neighbouring castles.

The outer defences, which were roughly oval and have been almost completely built over in modern times, are dominated by a massive donjon measuring 100 x 60 feet. On the ground floor is a chapel built at the turn of the 12th–13th centuries, and above it a twin-aisled hall.

History

1166–7. The early history of the site is obscure. The castle is first mentioned in connection with its capture by the ruler of Aleppo, Nûr ad-dîn, but the Franks must have done work on it at an earlier date. Safita is soon recaptured by the Franks and later passes into the keeping of the Templars, who renovate the castle after the earthquake of 1170.

1171. Another attack by Nûr ad-dîn causes renewed devastation.

1188. The castle, which has clearly undergone extensive rebuilding in the interval, successfully resists Saladin during his triumphal progress through Northern Syria.

1202. Restoration of the castle after yet another earthquake. The donjon in its present form probably dates from this period.

1218. Diversionary attack on the castle by Malik al-Ašraf of Aleppo, designed to harass the rear of the fifth Crusader army which is currently besieging Damietta.

1271. The castle falls into Arab hands after being briefly invested by the army of Sultan Baibars, who goes on from there to besiege Krak des Chevaliers.

The castle was still in a fairly good state of preservation at the end of the 19th century, but has been largely demolished and built over in the course of the small town's development.

Bibliography:
Rey, Arch. Militaire, 85-92 and Pl. 9;
Enlart, *Monuments II*, 89–93;
Deschamps, *Châteaux I*, 31, 85, 94 et seq., 106 et seq., 120 et seq.

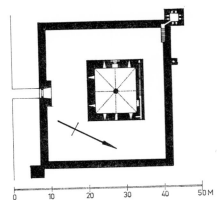

Plan 8: QAL'AT YAHMUR – CHASTEL ROUGE. *Ground-plan of castle, scale 1:1000. (Based on Deschamps, Châteaux I, 57.)*

QAL'AT YAHMUR   Plates 40–41

Frk. Chastel Rouge; Arab. Qal'at Yahmûr.

Description

Castle and village in the Syrian south coastal region, situated in the extreme southernmost spurs of the Nūsairî mountains. Originally part of a co-ordinated line of defence, the castle is in visual contact with Tortosa in the north and Arima in the south. It consists of a strong donjon enclosed by a single rectangular wall.

History

Excavations prove that the site was inhabited in ancient times. It never possessed very much importance at any period, and information about the castle is extremely scanty.

Early 12th century. The place is captured at some unspecified date by the Franks of Antioch. The Counts of Tripoli acquire it by marriage in 1112, though it was probably fortified earlier than this.

1177–8. Raymond III of Tripoli bestows the castle on the Hospitallers, compensating its former occupants, the Montolieu family, with a grant of land elsewhere.

1289. The castle is captured by the army of Sultan Qala'ûn. It is slightly altered during the Arab period by the annexing of two corner-towers to the outer wall.

Bibliography:
Deschamps, *Châteaux I*, 56 et seq., 106 et seq.;
J. Richard, *Le Comté de Tripoli sous la Dynastie Toulousaine (1102–1187)*, Paris 1945, pass.

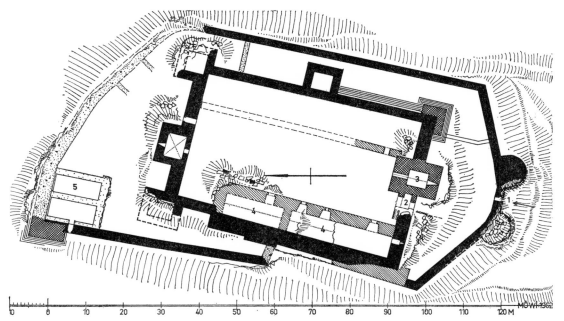

Plan 9: ARIMA. *Ground-plan of the upper fortress and inner citadel, scale 1:1000. Black, cross-hatched and hatched areas indicate different structural phases (undated). 1, Outer gate. 2, Main gate of inner citadel. 3, Small donjon. 4, Single-aisled, barrel-vaulted hall (destroyed). 5, Cisterns and exterior corner-tower. (Based on author's surveys.)*

ARIMA   Plates 42–43

Frk. Arima, Oraima, Areima, etc.; Arab. 'Areime, 'Oraimah, Qal'a 'Arîma.

Description

Ruined castle in the southern coastal region of Syria, situated on a ridge bordering the wide plain of the Nahr el-Kebîr, where it commands the entrance to the valley of the Nahr Abraš. It once formed part of a system of fortifications which extended from Tripoli to Tortosa.

Evidently built on the site of an earlier settlement, the castle consists of two parts: a spacious lower fortress, enclosed by a single perimeter wall and divided roughly in half by a cross-wall; and the more heavily fortified upper fortress in the north, which is separated from the rest of the precincts by a deep fosse. More or less in the centre of the upper fortress stands a rectangular citadel with corner-towers, enclosed by a simple walled forecourt which conforms to the lie of the land. The whole castle is badly dilapidated and has yet to be studied in detail.

History

1149. The early history of the site is unknown. The castle is first mentioned in connection with its transference from Tripolitanian ownership to Bertrand of Toulouse. It is later restored to Tripoli and subsequently acquired by the Templars.

1166–7. Arima is captured by Nûr ad-dîn of Aleppo, but seems to have been recaptured by the Franks very soon afterwards, because Arab sources refer to it as being in Frankish hands during the severe earthquake of 1170.

1171. Nûr ad-dîn inflicts further damage on the castle.

Arima's subsequent history is still obscure, but it probably remained a Templar possession until the end of Frankish rule.

Bibliography:
Deschamps, *Châteaux I*, 49 et seq., 85, 107, 120 et seq.;
Guide Bleu: Moyen-Orient, Paris 1965, 337.

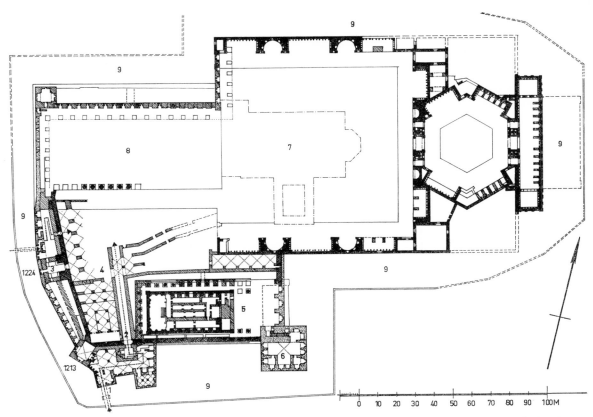

Plan 10: BA'ALBEK. *General plan of the converted temple precincts, scale 1:2000. Buildings of the Roman imperial era in black, buildings prior to the middle of the 12th century cross-hatched, buildings dating from the first half of the 13th century hatched, late 13th-century buildings stippled. 1, Barbican. 2, Inner south gate. 3, Old west gate. 4, Ruined mosque. 5, Temple of Bacchus with medieval additions. 6, Tower of Sultan Qala'ûn. 7, Byzantine church (demolished in the course of excavation). 8, Foundations of Temple of Jupiter. 9, Defensive ditches. (Based on Schulz – Winnefeld – Krencker, amplified by author.)*

BA'ALBEK

Plates 44–46

Gr. Heliopolis; Frk. Balbek, Maubec, etc;
Arab. Ba'albek, Ba'lbakk.

Description

Small township in the Beqâ' or highland plateau between the Lebanon and the Anti-Lebanon ranges, noted for its ancient temples. The large temple precincts, which date from various periods of the Roman Imperial era, were converted into a fortress and repeatedly improved during the Middle Ages by the addition of new perimeter walls and towers. Although archaeologists have only preserved the remains of these fortifications in so far as they do not obtrude on ancient buildings, Ba'albek – like Bosra (page 67) – provides an admirable demonstration of the way in which large edifices of the ancient world were put to use in the Middle Ages.

History

Already converted into a fortress during the Byzantine era, the former temple precincts changed hands several times after their initial capture by the Arabs in 637 and their devastation in 744. The place was briefly occupied by Byzantine invaders under Emperor John Tzimisces in 974, but by the time of the First Crusade, after passing from one Arab ruler to another, it was held by the Seljuk atabêgs of Damascus, first Duqâq ibn-Tutuš and then Atabêg Toghtekîn.

1110. The governor, a eunuch named Gümüštekîn al-Tâjî, negotiates with the Franks in an endeavour to cede the fortress to them and become an independent overlord. Since Ba'albek is an advanced outpost whose function is to guard the whole of the fertile Beqâ' from the Franks, Gümüštekîn is at once dismissed and the fortress entrusted to Bûrî, a son of the Atabêg of Damascus.

1136 or 1139. After dissension among Toghtekîn's heirs, Ba'albek is captured by Zengî, ruler of Aleppo, who bestows the governorship on Emir Nağm ad-dîn Ayyûb, father of Salâh ed-dîn (Saladin). The defences are extensively improved at this period.

1170. The fortress sustains severe damage by earthquake. Saladin captures it a short while later, in 1174, and after his death in 1193 it passes to his grandnephew, Bahrâm-Shâh.

1213–24. Bahrâm-Shâh improves the fortress by adding several towers.

1260. The Mongols capture and devastate Ba'albek during their withdrawal from Syria, but it is repaired and improved shortly afterwards by Sultan Qala'ûn, who constructs the large artillery-tower adjoining the Temple of Bacchus, reinforces the west wall, and adds a barbican to the south gate.

Ba'albek lost its importance in the course of the Middle Ages, and no further building was carried out. More severe earthquake damage occurred in 1759. Excavation of the ancient ruins began early in the 20th century.

Bibliography:
Enc. Isl. I, 564–6 (M. von Sobernheim 1913);
Enc. Isl. (2)I, 1000–1 (J. Sourdel – Thomine 1960);
Schulz – Winnefeld – Krencker and others (publ. by Th. Wiegand);
Baalbek, Ergebnisse der Ausgrabungen und Untersuchungen 1898–1905, Vol. III, Berlin 1925.

SHEIZAR

Plates 47–49

Gr. Sizara, To Sézer; Arab. Cheizar, Sheizar, Saizar, etc.

Description

Castle and village in Central Syria, situated near an ancient bridging-place and ford on the upper reaches of the Orontes, north-west of Hamâ. The castle stands beside the river on a long narrow ridge, separated from the rocky slope adjoining it in the south by a deep fosse. Rising almost vertically from this ditch is the front wall of the donjon, a massive edifice with two interior storeys and a large roof platform – undoubtedly the product of several building periods. The walls which skirted the edge of the ridge on each of the castle's longer flanks have largely collapsed, and all that has survived is the northernmost tip of the castle, a sloping revetment, and the stoutly constructed gate.

Although the villagers have moved out of the interior of the castle, it has not received the care and attention due to an ancient monument, and is bound to deteriorate still further.

History

Originally founded as a Seleucid military settlement, Sheizar's convenient proximity to a ford endowed it with local importance for many centuries. It also played an important role in the struggles between Emperor Nicephorus Phocas and the Arab emirs of Northern Syria, changing hands several times during this period.

Late 11th century. Sheizar is the residence of the Munqidits, a dynasty of Arab emirs, and enjoys considerable importance as an offensive base used by the Arab rulers of Northern Syria.

Early 12th century. The castle is several times unsuccessfully besieged by the Franks.

1138. Sheizar is invested by John II Comnenus of Byzantium (1118–43), who is soon forced to abandon the siege in default of adequate Frankish support.

1157. An earthquake badly damages the castle, killing the emir and his entire family. The Franks attempt to occupy the now defenceless castle but are forestalled by the Ismaelites of Masyâd.

1158. The Franks launch another fruitless attack on Sheizar, which is occupied c. 1160 by Nûr ad-dîn of Aleppo.

1233. Large dated inscription on the donjon suggests that it may have been built at this time.

1260–1. The castle is damaged by Mongol invaders but restored immediately after their defeat at the hands of Sultan Baibars.

1290. An inscription records the building of the large gate by Sultan Qala'ûn.

Although in use until the end of Arab rule, the castle slowly falls into decay after the Ottoman conquest of Syria, and is now a ruin.

Bibliography:
Enc. Isl. IV, 309–311 (E. Honigmann 1934);
v. Berchem – Fatio, *Voyage I*, 177–188.

QAL'AT EL-MUDIQ   Plates 50–51

Ancient name Apamea, whence Frk. Afamia, La Famie, etc.; Arab. Afâmiya, since c. 17th century Qal'at el-Mudiq.

Description

Fortified township in the south-western spurs of the North Syrian highland plateau, situated on an isolated rocky knoll above the marshy valley of the Orontes.

The medieval settlement probably occupied the site of the acropolis of ancient Apamea and, thus, the site of the earliest settlement, since the hill on which the modern township stands undoubtedly owes part of its present elevation to the debris left by centuries of inhabitants. The medieval defences consisted of a simple perimeter wall reinforced with rectangular corner-towers, the main gate in the south being more heavily fortified by the addition of two large towers. The fortifications were almost entirely constructed of material taken from ancient buildings.

History

540. The ancient city is destroyed by Chosroes I of Persia and loses its erstwhile importance. After the Arab conquest it becomes the seat of a petty local overlord. The ancient ruins are later systematically stripped of material for the construction of Samarra.

1100. Bohemond of Antioch fails in his first attempt to seize this strategic point, but inter-Arab rivalries soon encourage him to try again.

1106. The town falls to Bohemond after a protracted siege. It becomes an important offensive base for Frankish expeditions into the Arab hinterland.

1149. Recapture of the town by Nûr ad-dîn of Aleppo.

1157. The fortifications are badly damaged by a severe earthquake and (possibly) occupied by the Franks for a short time thereafter.

1170. More earthquake damage. Extensive reconstruction presumed to have been carried out by Nûr ad-dîn.

The town remains in Muslim hands under a series of Arab rulers. Its defences are further improved in the years 1205 and 1256 (according to inscriptions), since it is now a base for Arab attacks on Frankish territory. Qal'at el-Mudîq loses all its military importance after the 14th–15th centuries and is now a modest country township, having survived almost unchanged until the present day.

Bibliography:
Enc. Isl. I, 153 (Fr. Buhl 1913);
Enc. Isl. (2)I, 221 (H. A. R. Gibb 1960);
v. Berchem – Fatio, *Voyage I*, 188–194.

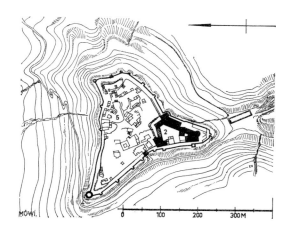

Plan 11: QAL'AT EL-MARQAB. *Site-plan of castle, scale 1:10,000. 1, Main gate. 2, Inner fortress. 3, Southern outworks. 4, North-west corner-tower. 5, Ruins of former village. (Based on aerial photographs and author's survey.)*

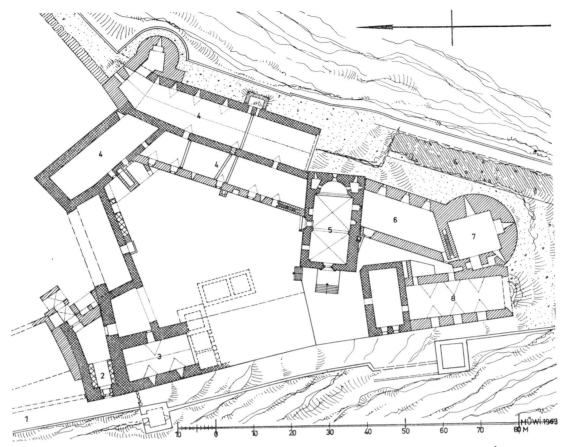

Plan 12: QAL'AT EL-MARQAB. *Ground-plan of inner fortress, scale 1:1000. 1, Forecourt between outer and inner gates. 2 and 3, Vaulted substructure of demolished chapterhouse (?). 4, Magazine chambers. 5, Castle chapel. 6, Large two-storeyed hall with adjacent donjon. 7 and 8, Hall. (Based on author's survey sketches.)*

MARQAB

Plates 52–61

Gr. Markappos, Marchapin; Frk. Margat, Margathum, Margant, etc.; Arab. el-Marqab, Qal'at Marqab.

Description

Castle on the Syrian coast near the small harbour town of Bâniyâs, situated on the summit of a rocky spur which juts close to the sea. The extensive fortified site consists of a strong inner citadel and a more spacious outer fortress – probably densely inhabited at one time – enclosed by a partially double perimeter wall interspersed with numerous towers of varying size and shape. The inner citadel, a roughly triangular castle with a double ring of

walls, lies at the southern tip of the site and is separated from the outer fortress by a wide fosse. The outer walls are only reinforced by isolated semicircular and rectangular bastions. They culminate in the south in some 13th-century outworks, built after the Arab conquest as a substitute for earlier defences which had been destroyed. The outer walls of the citadel are an extension of those of the outer fortress. The core of the citadel, a stoutly constructed circular tower with a diameter of approximately 72 feet, also faces south. This tower is adjoined on two sides by multi-storeyed buildings containing large vaulted halls. In the centre of the citadel stands a largish chapel which divides it into two courtyards of unequal size. Grouped round the larger northern courtyard are magazines and stables. Access to the whole fortress is through a stout gate-tower in the west face of the outer perimeter wall, and from there through a forecourt into the main gatehouse, which comprises a succession of chambers.

The fortifications are comparatively well preserved because the village which existed within the outer fortress until the 19th century was abandoned; but the castle, which dates from several different periods, has yet to be systematically surveyed and investigated.

History

1062. Arab sources record the building of a castle by a chieftain of the mountain tribes resident in the district.

1104. The place is briefly occupied by Byzantine troops commanded by John Cantacuzenus during the struggle for Lattaqia. Thereafter (according to Arab sources) it is restored to Arab possession.

1116–18. After protracted negotiations, the lord of Marqab, Ibn Muḥriz, cedes the castle to Roger, Prince of Antioch, in exchange for another estate. Roger gives Marqab in fee to the Mansoer family.

1157, 1170 and 1186. Earthquakes wreck the castle, necessitating repairs which prove too much for the Mansoers' resources. In 1186 the castle is handed over to the Hospitallers in return for an annual revenue of 2000 gold Bezants, payable to its last owner, Bertrand de Margat.

1188. Saladin passes very close to Margat during his advance through Northern Syria but does not attack it, presumably because its new masters have carried out prompt and extensive repairs.

1204–5. The castle is besieged by the Sultan of Aleppo, al-Malik Zâhir Gâzî, who destroys a few of the towers in the perimeter wall. (The Hospitallers use Margat as a base for their frequent raids on Arab-held territory.)

1269–71. Renewed Arab attacks. The fall of the neighbouring castle of Krak (1271) compels the knights of Margat to give up part of their lands and undertake not to carry out any more work on the castle.

1285. The castle is besieged by an army under Sultan Qala'ûn. The south face is undermined and bombarded, and the south outer tower (known as the Tour de l'Espérance or Tour de l'Eperon) collapses. Confronted by the threat of further sapping, the knights surrender in return for a guarantee of safe-conduct.

The Arabs deliberate as to whether the castle should be dismantled or rebuilt. In view of its important strategic position, rebuilding is started under Emir Saif ad-dîn Balabân aṭ-Tabbâhî.

The castle remained one of the country's principal strongholds in the 14th-15th centuries, when it served as a place of detention for deposed governors. Minor alterations were carried out so as to accommodate the small Turkish garrison which was stationed there in more recent times.

Bibliography:
Enc. Isl. III, 319–320 (E. Honigmann 1936);
Rey, *Arch. Militaire*, 19–38;
v. Berchem – Fatio, *Voyage I*, 292–320;
Enlart, *Monuments II*, 441–3;
Comte Chandon de Briailles, 'Lignages d'Outremer: Les Seigneurs de Margat', in: *Syria 25*, 1946/48, 231–258;
Fedden-Thomson, passim and Pl. 20–28.

QAL'AT AJLUN   Plates 62–65

Arab. Qal'at 'Aǧlûn, also Qal'at er-Rabad.

Description

Castle in North-West Jordan, some thirty miles north-west of the capital, 'Ammân, in the outlying spurs of the massif which adjoins the Jordan Valley in the east. Built on a rocky knoll and situated at more than 3000 feet above sea level, the castle commands an excellent view of the entire Jordan Valley and the mountain slopes opposite. A fosse separates it from the mountainous terrain surrounding it, which is not unduly precipitous.

The castle came into being at two periods, and is compact in design. The upper fortress, an irregular rectangle with four corner-towers, is bounded in the north and south-east by courtyards, originally open to the sky but densely built over at a later stage. The fosse which surrounds the whole site is hewn deep into the solid rock. The castle is fairly well preserved.

History

1184–5. Emir 'Izz ed-dîn Usâma founds the castle to safeguard the hitherto ill-protected south-west flank of the Damascus area and the vital line of communication between Damascus and Cairo (the so-called Darb al-Haǧǧ), also as a counterweight to

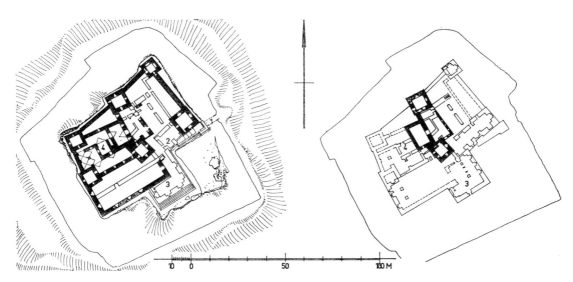

Plan 13: QAL'AT AJLUN. *Ground-plan of the castle, scale 1:2000 (ground floor left, upper floor right). Portions dating from 1184–5 in black, 1214–15 additions unshaded. 1, Main access. 2, Inner gate-chamber. 3, South tower. 4, Inner fortress. (Based on C. N. Johns.)*

the castle of Belvoir. Arab sources state that the site was previously occupied by a monastery.

1211. The castle is besieged because its master declined to swear allegiance to the new Sultan after Saladin's death. It is given to Aybak ibn'Abdallâh.

1214–15. The new owner carries out extensive structural improvements, strengthening the south face and roofing in the open courtyard.

Mid-13th century. Having lost its strategic importance after the Arab victory at Hattîn, the castle is used merely as a supply depot. Although restored by Sultan Baibars after its destruction by the Mongols in 1260, Qal'at Ajlun ceases to play a major role. It becomes the home of a handful of families and remains so until the 19th century.

Bibliography:
Enc. Isl. (2) I, 214 (D. Sourdel 1960);
C. N. Johns, Medieval 'Ajlun', in: *Quarterly of the Department of Antiquities in Palestine*, I 1931, 21–33.

KRAK DES CHEVALIERS Plates 66–83

Frk. Crac, Crac de l'Opital; Lat Cratum, castrum Crati; Arab. Ḥiṣn al-Akrâd, Qal'at al-Ḥiṣn, etc.; the accepted modern designation is Krak des Chevaliers.

Description

Castle and village in the spurs of the Nuṣairî mountains in Southern Syria. Favourably situated on a hill-top over 2100 feet up and surrounded on all sides by moderately steep gradients, it is in direct visual communication with the neighbouring fortress of Chastel Blanc (Safita).

Krak has been partially restored in recent years and is one of the best preserved and most impressive examples of fortification in the Frankish Levant. Although not the largest castle of the Crusader epoch in terms of walled area, it is certainly the most grandiose. In its present state, it embodies several fairly major alterations made during the Arab period.

Isolated from the ridge which stretches away to the south by a fosse hewn out of the rock, the castle consists of two concentric rings of fortifications linked by a long, ramped entry by which mounted men could ascend from the outer gatehouse to the inner courtyard.

The outer ring, polygonal but approximately oval in shape, consists of a wall containing several defensive galleries and reinforced with semicircular bastions. The small subsidiary gate in the north face is guarded by two closely adjacent bastions. The east face was considerably altered during the Arab period. This flank, which enjoys somewhat better natural protection than the others, is guarded by three small rectangular bastions of which one contains the main entrance. The sector most extensively altered by the Arabs is the south face, or main defensive front, where widespread siege damage had to be made good. Like the long west face, this originally consisted of a curtain-wall protected by semicircular bastions and a continuous machicolated gallery, but was reinforced after 1285 by Sultan Qala'ûn's massive tower.

Within the outer ring of fortifications is a forecourt, and, in the south, a deep rock-hewn fosse which also served as a reservoir.

From the moat rises the main, southern, face of the upper fortress: three massive semicircular towers which overtop the outer defences and seem to grow naturally out of the steep revetment. Behind this splendidly faced revetment are two vaulted defensive galleries which are accessible from the large chambers on the ground floor of the upper fortress. All three towers contain large vaulted chambers disposed on several floors, and the circular southwest corner-tower houses a particularly well-appointed room known as the 'Logis du Maître'. The rooms between the towers have been destroyed. The two longer flanks of the upper fortress display no special features. In the west stands a semicircular tower which was added to at several stages, and in the east the apse of the castle chapel projects slightly above the level of the walls. The rectangular tower at the northern tip of the upper fortress has a multi-tiered arrangement of arches which lends particular charm to the exterior façade.

Large sections of the courtyards in the interior of the castle are covered by massive vaults which divide their surface area – originally level, one presumes – into a number of terraces. In the courtyard, opposite the chapel, stands the delightful mid-13th-century Great Hall and cloister.

History

1031. A castle is founded by the Emir of Homs and occupied by a Kurdish military colony. Although the site was probably inhabited before this, nothing is known of its early history.

1099. Krak is briefly occupied by Crusaders on their way to Jerusalem.

1109. Tancred of Antioch captures Krak after previously besieging it unsuccessfully in 1102.

1112. The castle is acquired by the Counts of Tripoli.

1115. It is briefly besieged by Alp Arslan, Sultan of Aleppo.

1142. Count Raymond II of Tripoli cedes Krak to the Hospitallers and compensates the former tenant, Guillaume de Cratum, with a grant of land elsewhere. The defences are extensively rebuilt after this change of ownership and the ensuing earthquake of 1157.

1163 and 1167. Arab attacks on Krak are repelled.

1169–70. After further severe damage has been inflicted by an earthquake, a second phase of construction begins with financial assistance from King Vladislas II of Bohemia. The chapel dates from this period.

1188. Saladin besieges Krak unsuccessfully for a month.

1201–2. Further earthquake damage heralds a third structural phase which produces the outer ring of defences, the large talus in the south, and the magazine situated behind the south face.

At this period, Krak plays an important role as an offensive base for Hospitaller-led raids on Arab territory, but is itself subjected to several attacks by the rulers of Aleppo (1207, 1218, 1229, and 1252).

1267. After the land east of Krak has been largely evacuated by the Franks in the face of the threat from Sultan Baibar's army, the Sultan launches his first attack on the district of Krak itself, capturing

Plan 14: KRAK DES CHEVALIERS. *Composite general ground-plan, all levels, scale 1:1000. 12th-century portions in black, 13th-century additions cross-hatched, additions subsequent to the middle of the 13th century hatched, post-1271 alterations unshaded. 1, North gate. 2, North tower. 3, Castle chapel. 4, Great Hall and cloister. 5, Magazine. 6, Substructure of the three south towers. 7, Lower main gate. 8, Barrier in passage-way. 9, Upper main gate. 10, Inner gate. 11, Stables and magazine. 12, Tower of Sultan Qala'ûn. (Based on Deschamps, Châteaux I.)*

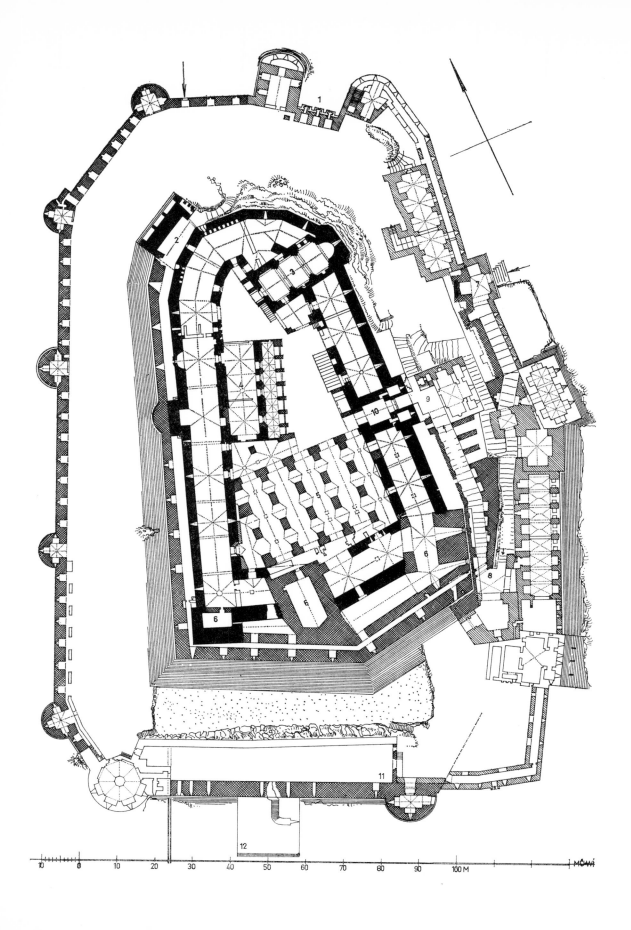

10   0   10   20   30   40   50   60   70   80   90   100 M

three castles and sixteen fortified towers in the vicinity.

1270. Sultan Baibars marches on Krak once more.

1271. A formal siege begins. Lavish use of siege-engines and ordnance forces Krak into submission after little more than a month. On 8 April the knights surrender in return for safe-conduct to Tripoli.

The castle is at once put into commission again by the Arabs. Two towers are constructed on the south side, and the new governor, Ṣarim ad-dîn Qâimâz, carries out extensive repairs under the unremitting supervision of the Sultan himself.

1285. Construction of the large rectangular tower projecting from the south face of the outer wall. The inscription on the tower attributes it to Sultan Qala'ûn.

1301–2. Damage caused by heavy falls of rain necessitates repairs to the upper fortress.

Krak was still in use during the late Middle Ages and in modern times. It was uninhabited and still almost intact in the early 1800s, but the growth of a small village in the ruins at the end of the century inflicted widespread damage on the surviving fabric. The site was subsequently acquired by the French government, and restoration work has been in progress ever since 1927.

Bibliography:
Rey, *Arch. Militaire*, 39 et seq;
v. Berchem – Fatio, *Voyage I*, 135–163;
Enlart, *Monuments II*, 93–9;
Deschamps, *Châteaux I*, containing full bibliographical data;
Fedden-Thomson, 76–82 and Pl. 38–50 (some of which amplify the plans given here).

BEAUFORT
Plate 84

Frk. Beaufort, Belfort, Belliforte, etc.; Arab Qal'at eš-Šeqîf Arnûn.

Description

Castle in Southern Lebanon, situated on a steep 2200-foot-high ridge opposite the Nahr al-Litani. Like the castle of Subeibe, with which it is in visual communication, it commands the southern approaches to the fertile Beqâ' plateau. The upper fortress, which has a large donjon and a massive wall constructed of boss-and-margin stonework, stands on a projecting knob of rock, while the lower fortress adjoins it on a narrow rocky shelf to the east. The castle precincts are entirely separated from the surrounding plateau, which was once inhabited, by a fosse hewn out of the solid rock.

History

1139. King Fulk captures the stronghold of Qal'at eš-Šeqîf from Emir Šehâb ed-dîn and bestows it on the feudal seigneur of Sagette (Saida). The fortress is strengthened by the addition of a donjon and a stout outer wall.

1187–90. Beaufort does not yield after the Frankish defeat at Hattîn, but is vigorously besieged by Arab troops from April 1189 onwards and simultaneously improved by the Franks. After a siege lasting about a year, the garrison is starved into submission.

The castle's new Arab masters at once embark on further improvements (a polygonal hall at the northern tip of the upper fortress, parts of the lower fortress, and a large corner-tower and revetment designed to strengthen the south face).

1240. Under the terms of a treaty between the Franks and Sultan Ṣâliḥ Isma'îl of Damascus, Beaufort is restored to Frankish ownership but has to be taken from its refractory garrison by force.

Further additions are made to the castle, among them the chapel (?) in the upper fortress. It is once more held by the seigneurs of Sagette.

1260. Julien de Sagette is compelled to sell Beaufort to the Templars, who augment its defences. Their main contribution is an outwork on the plateau to the south, designed to hinder the use of siege-engines against the castle.

1268. Sultan Baibars besieges the castle and forces it to surrender after barely a fortnight by using massed engines. The castle is renovated by its new governor, Emir Ṣârim ed-dîn Qâimâz Qafûrî.

Later abandoned on account of its remote position, the castle has preserved its medieval, though ruined, state. Because of its proximity to the Israel border, photographs may be taken only under strict military supervision.

Bibliography:
Deschamps, *Châteaux II*, 176–208,
with full bibliographical data and plans.

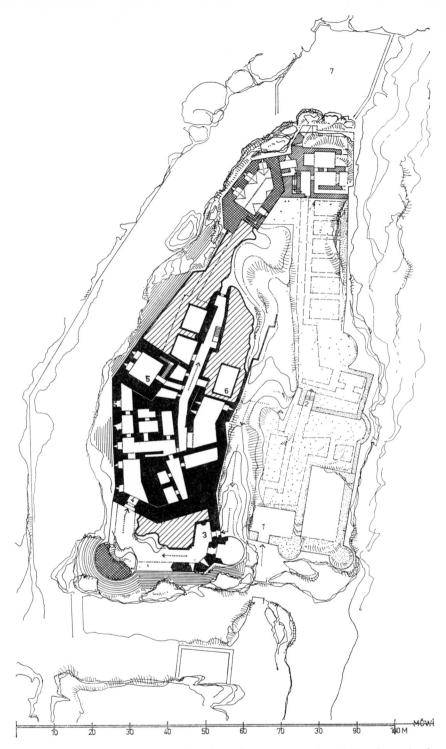

Plan 15: BEAUFORT. *General ground-plan of castle, scale 1:1000. Portions dating from the first two Frankish building periods in black, Arab additions (1190–1240) cross-hatched, further Arab additions (post-1240) closely hatched, premises lying beneath soil and rock widely hatched. 1, Outer gate-chamber of lower fortress. 2, Egress through underground gateway into courtyard of lower fortress. 3, Outer gate of upper fortress. 4, Inner gate of upper fortress. 5, Donjon. 6, Substructure of chapel (?). 7, Cistern in castle fosse. (Based on Deschamps, Châteaux II.)*

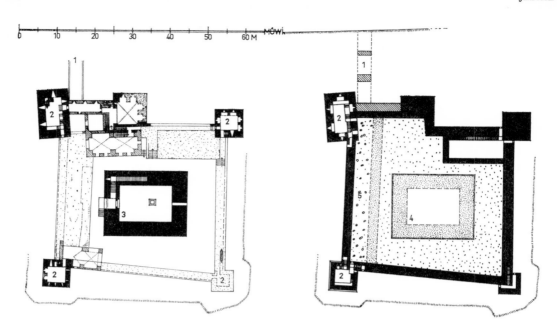

Plan 17: JEBAIL – GIBLET. *Ground-plans of castle (ground floor left, basement right), scale 1:1000. Frankish portions in black, Arab and Turkish additions hatched. 1, Approach (via bridge). 2, Corner-towers with side gates. 3, Donjon. 4, Cistern in basement of donjon. 5, Rubble-filled vault (magazine). (Based on Deschamps, Châteaux I, 50, and author's measurements.)*

JEBAIL   Plates 85–87

*Gr. Byblos; Frk. Giblet, Gibelet etc.;
Arab. Djebail, Ğubayl, etc.*

Description

Town and castle on the Lebanese coast with a small but well-protected harbour, built on the site of the ancient Phoenician sea-port of Byblos. Unlike the original settlement, the town entirely encloses the small harbour and is itself surrounded by a simple perimeter wall interspersed with towers. In the south-east corner of the small township stands the castle. Measuring 58/72 feet and built of massive boss-and-margin stonework, the tower is enclosed on all sides by a curtain wall reinforced with smallish corner-towers. The gate is guarded by an extra tower in the centre of the north face.

The castle underwent minor changes during the Turkish occupation.

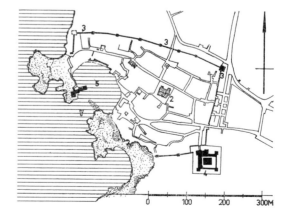

Plan 16: JEBAIL – GIBLET. *Town plan, scale 1:10,000. 1, Harbour fort. 2, Church of St John. 3, Town gate. 4, Castle. 5, Harbour. (Based on M. Dunand, Fouilles de Byblos I, Paris 1939.)*

History

1103. After capturing Tortosa (Ṭarṭûs), Raymond de St Gilles besieges Giblet with the help of Genoese ships and takes the town by storm on 28 April. Genoa receives one-third of Giblet for services rendered, and in 1109, after the capture of Tripoli, acquires the whole town. Giblet is entrusted to a Genoese nobleman, Ugo Umbriaco, who initially administers it on behalf of his native city. His descendants retain the town as an hereditary domain.

The earliest portions of the castle probably date from the 12th century.

1170. The town is damaged by an earthquake.

1188. Saladin acquires town and castle as ransom for Hugues III de Giblet.

1190. Tidings of the approach of Emperor Frederick I (Barbarossa) and his army cause Saladin to dismantle Giblet's fortifications.

1197–8. Guy I de Giblet regains possession of his family seat and rebuilds its defences.

1369. The town is raided by Cypriot ships from Famagusta.

Jebail played no further part in the history of the country. Minor alterations were subsequently carried out for the benefit of the small garrison quartered there during the Turkish period.

Bibliography:
v. Berchem-Fatio, *Voyage I*, 105–113;
Enlart, *Monuments II*, 116–124;
E. G. Rey, 'Les Seigneurs de Giblet', in:
Rev. Or. Lat. 3, 1895, 398–442 (family history);
Enc. Isl. (2) II, 582–3 (D. Sourdel 1963).

HARIM   Plates 88–89

Frk. Castrum Harenc, Harrench, Harrem, etc.;
Arab. Ḥârim.

Description

Castle and township in Northern Syria, situated in the western spurs of the Ǧebel Barîša on the edge of the plain surrounding Lake Amq and commanding the main road between Antioch and Aleppo.

The castle stands on a rocky mound which has been artificially elevated by centuries of human habitation, and was probably protected on all sides by a fosse which had to be hewn deep into the rock on the nort-east flank. Large areas of the uniform slope surrounding it were revetted. The fortifications were closely adapted to the terrain. They consisted of a curtain wall, now badly dilapidated but once reinforced with stout towers, and, in the east of the roughly oval site, a large rectangular 'citadel' of which very little has survived.

History

Mid-10th century. A small fortress is built at Ḥârim following the reconquest of the North Syrian area by the Byzantine Emperor Nicephorus Phocas of Byzantium (963–969) and the fall of Antioch.

1085. Ḥârim and Antioch fall to the Seljuk army of Süleymân ibn-Qutulmiš.

1097–8. The castle threatens the rear of the Crusader army besieging Antioch, and is captured during the winter.

1149. Ḥârim is briefly occupied by Nûr ad-dîn of Aleppo.

1164. Recaptured by Nûr ad-dîn, Ḥârim remains in Arab hands despite several Frankish counterattacks.

1199. The defences are strengthened by al-Malik Ẓâhir Gâzî, ruler of Aleppo, who builds new towers (among them, probably, the 'citadel') and revets the escarpments. Work continues under his successor.

Late 13th century. Ḥârim is restored after being ravaged by the Mongols in 1260 and 1271, but has not possessed any importance since the late Middle Ages.

Bibliography:
Enc. Isl. II, 284;
Guide Bleu: Moyen Orient, Paris 1956, 315;
v. Berchem – Fatio, *Voyage I*, 229–238;
Cl. Cahen, *La Syrie du Nord à l'époque des Croisades*, Paris 1940, pass.

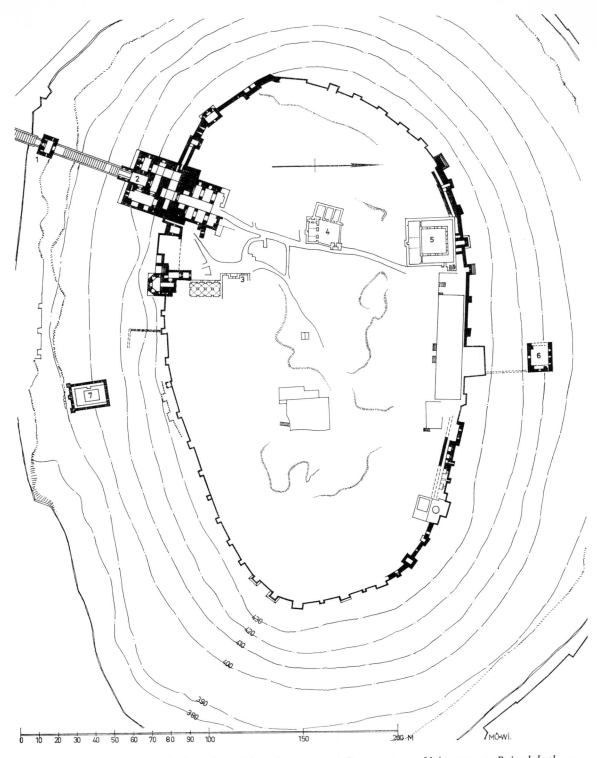

Plan 18: ALEPPO. *General plan of citadel, scale 1:2000, 1, Outer gate. 2, Main gate. 3, Ruined bath. 4, Small mosque (so-called Mosque of Abraham, built in 1162 by Nûr ad-dîn). 5, Large mosque (built in 1210 by Malik az-Zâhir). 6, North outer tower. 7, South outer tower (above remains of an earlier citadel wall). (Based on a survey by the Service des Antiquités de Syrie and author's observations.)*

ALEPPO

Plates 90–91

Arab. Ḥalab.

Description and History

Capital of Northern Syria and an inhabited site for thousands of years. The original nucleus of the urban area is the large 'Tell' in the middle of the modern city, which was converted into a citadel during the Middle Ages. Like the ancient city, the medieval residential quarter occupied the area between the citadel and the small river Queiq, a piece of ground which slopes away gently towards the west.

By the 10th century, Aleppo had become the capital of an independent petty state ruled by a Hamdanid overlord named Sayf ad-dawla. In 962, after his defeat by the Byzantine general (later emperor) Nicephorus Phocas, the city was totally destroyed. Towards the end of the 11th century it came into the possession of Seljuk princes. Incessant squabbling in the Muslim camp led, in the early years of the 12th century, to Crusader incursions into the vicinity of the city itself, but this threat was dispelled by Atabêg Zengî's assumption of power in 1128. The city still retained its importance as the seat of successive local rulers and the commercial centre of Northern Syria, but was no longer militarily involved in the struggle with the Franks.

Work on the fortifications, which steadily deteriorated after 962 and suffered severe damage in the great earthquake of 1157, was begun under Nûr ad-dîn shortly after the earthquake and continued, with interruptions, until the 13th century. Under Saladin's son, Sultan aẓ-Ẓâhir Gâzî, large sections of the town defences were completely rebuilt and adapted to the changed requirements of siege warfare, as were the fortifications of the citadel, notably the main gate (1208–13). Originally composed of two towers with a gateway between them, this was restored and substantially altered between 1404 and 1406 so as to remedy damage inflicted by Hulagu's Mongols in 1260 and Timur's in 1400. The two separate towers were linked by a large hall. The last Mameluke Sultans restored the citadel during their struggle with the Ottoman Turks, the outer gate being begun by Sultan Qânṣûh al-Ghûrî in 1504.

Bibliography:
Enc. Isl. II, 241–251 (Sobernheim-Herzfeld 1927); J. Sauvaget, *Alep. Essai sur le developpement d'une grande ville syrienne...* Paris 1941 (text and pl.); E. Herzfeld, *Matériaux pour un Corpus Inscr. Arabicarum*, Part II: *Syrie du Nord: Inscriptions et monuments d'Alep*, Cairo 1954–55 (MIFAO 36–38).

BOSRA

Plates 92–94

Ancient and Frk. Bostra; Arab. Boṣrâ, Boṣrâ Eski-Šâm.

Description

Town on the edge of the Haurân in Southern Syria, once the capital of the Roman province of Arabia. The largest of the numerous ancient buildings to have survived there is the Roman theatre. At Boṣrâ, as in many other places, this was converted into a citadel during the Middle Ages. Several tiers of cisterns and magazines were built into the old *cavea* or auditorium, and the exterior façade, formerly open, was fortified with walls and towers.

History

634. After being devastated by the Persians in 613 and permanently robbed of its erstwhile political status, the town is recaptured by the Arabs and its theatre converted into a stronghold.

1088–90. The first towers are built at the northeast corner of the citadel.

Early 12th century. The ruler of Boṣrâ, Aytekîn, joins forces with the Franks against the Fatimids. He and his successors make several attempts to cede the town to the Franks, but, despite their efforts and despite Frankish attacks in 1147 and 1151, Boṣrâ remains in Arab hands. The citadel begins to assume its present form under Saladin.

Early 13th century. The citadel's nine towers, which are precisely dated by inscriptions, come into being between 1211 and 1251.

1260–61. The town is devastated by the Mongols and restored by Sultan Baibars. Being situated deep in the Arab hinterland, the town plays no further part in the military conflicts of the late Frankish period.

The Roman theatre has been excavated in recent times and those parts of the fortress which lie within the *cavea* have been demolished.

Bibliography:

Enc. Isl. I, 797 (Fr. Buhl 1913);
Enc. Isl. (2) I, 1314–16 (A. Abel 1960);
E. Ouéchek – S. A. Mougdad, *Bosra, Guide historique et archéologique*, Damascus 1954;
A. Abel, 'La citadelle Ayyubite de Bosra-Eski Châm', in: *Annales Archéologiques de Syrie 6*, 1956, 95–138.

Plan 19: BOSRA. *Town plan, scale 1:10,000. 1, Ancient town wall. 2, Roman theatre and citadel. 3, Roman baths. 4, So-called Palace of Trajan. 5, Ruins of cathedral. 6, So-called Basilica of Bahîra. 7, Mabrak an-Nâqa Mosque and cemetery. 8, Mosque of Omar (founded 780 by Caliph Yazîd II). 9, Medrese Abû'l-Fidâ (1225) and mausoleum. 10, Birket al-Hajj (open cistern). 11, Former stadium. (Based on E. Ouéchek and S. A. Mougdad.)*

MASYAF

Plate 95

Frk. Messiat; Arab. Maṣyâd, Maṣyâf, etc.

Description

Castle and township in Western Central Syria, situated in rolling hill country in the eastern spurs of the Ğebel en-Nuṣayrîye. The small town is enclosed by a simple curtain wall. At its eastern end is the castle, whose outer walls follow the outlines of the elongated rocky knoll on which it stands. Admirably protected by a systematic use of topographical features, it is an extremely compact citadel consisting of an upper ward enclosed by an outer fortress whose individual components display a wide variety of building techniques and hail from widely scattered periods.

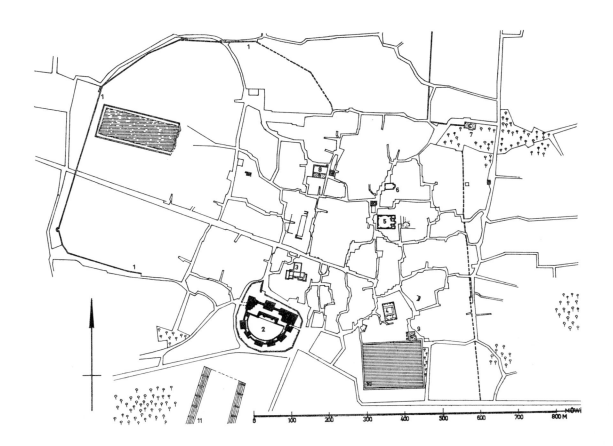

History

1099. Already in existence in Byzantine times, the castle is held by a branch of the Mirdasids during the first Frankish expedition.

1103. Reputed to be in Frankish hands briefly.

1109–10. A treaty between the Count of Tripoli and the Atabêg of Damascus grants Maṣyâf immunity from Frankish raids in return for tribute.

1127. Sold to the Banû Munqidh, who are tricked into relinquishing it to the Ismaelites (Assassins). In company with Qadmûs, the castle becomes the seat of Šeikh el-Ǧebel, Grand Master of the Order.

1176. Saladin besieges the castle in retaliation for two attempts on his life by the Assassins, but the parties are soon reconciled and the siege is raised.

c. 1220. According to an inscription, new building and maintenance work is carried out in the castle's interior by Kemâl ad-dîn, Syrian Grand Master of the Order of Assassins.

1249. A town gate is built by Tâǧ ad-dîn Abu'l-Futûḫ, a Persian from Alamût, headquarters of the Order.

1260. Maṣyâf is captured, briefly occupied, and devastated by the Mongols, who are forced to withdraw again after their defeat at 'Ain Ǧâlût.

1270. The castle is captured and occupied in the course of a campaign to suppress the Order waged by Sultan Baibars. It belongs first to the district of Ḥiṣn al-Akrâd and later to the province of Tripoli.

Having played a minor role in domestic disputes between the local population and the Ismaelites in 1808, the castle was subsequently occupied by the French, cleared, and partially restored.

Bibliography:

Enc. Isl. III, 465–67 (E. Honigmann 1936);
Deschamps, *Châteaux I* (Plate V b);
Fedden – Thomson, Pl. 37 (aerial photograph);
Marshall G. Hodgson, *The Order of Assassins*, 'sGravenhage 1955;
M. van Berchem, 'Epigraphie des Assassins', in: *Journ. Asiat.* Ser. 9, Vol. 9, 481 et seq.

SAIDA – SIDON   Plates 96–97

Gr. – Lat. Sidon; Frk. Sagette, Sayette, Seyde, etc.; Arab. Ṣaidâ'.

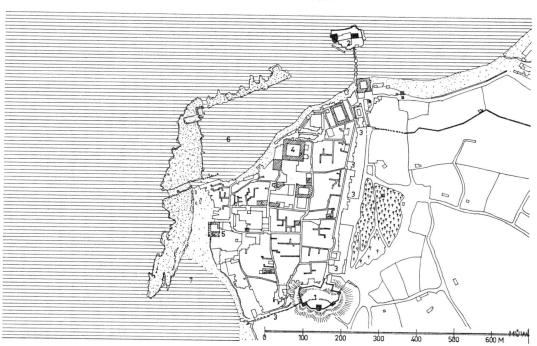

Plan 20: SAIDA – SIDON. *Town plan as at mid-19th century, scale 1:10'000. 1, Mainland fortress (Qal'at al-Mu'azza). 2, Harbour fort (Qal'at al-baḥr). 3, Presumed circuit of medieval town wall. 4, Khân el-Fransâwî. 5, Large mosque. 6, Main harbour. 7, So-called Egyptian Harbour. (Based on Guide Bleu and old town plans.)*

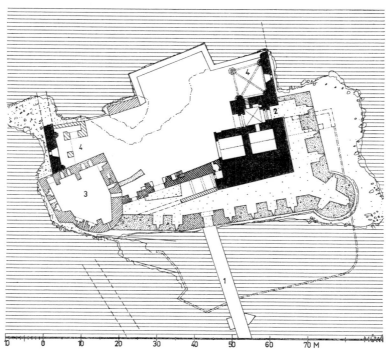

Plan 21: SAIDA – SIDON. *Ground-plan of harbour fort, scale 1:1000. Frankish structural phases (13th-century) black and cross-hatched, Arab additions hatched. 1, Restored bridge. 2, Old main gate. 3, Main tower. 4, Ruins of Great Hall on seaward side. (Based on author's survey supplemented (broken lines) by Deschamps, Châteaux II, 230.)*

Description

Town and fortress on the southern coast of the Lebanon, formerly the site of Sidon, a Phoenician seaport which enjoyed many centuries of importance. Situated on a broad spit of land projecting not far into the sea, the town possessed a harbour which was sheltered by reefs and man-made moles and protected against naval attack by a sea-fort.

The town used to be enclosed by walls and guarded on the landward side by a citadel (the Qal'at al-Mu'azza) which dominated it from the brow of a low hill. Nothing survives of the citadel save one tower and isolated sections of wall. The town walls have also disappeared. The sea-fort, which underwent numerous alterations during the Turkish period, has been extensively restored in recent years, but not all its structural components are historically identifiable.

History

1110. Having been blockaded since 1106, Şaidâ is formally besieged and captured with the aid of a Norwegian fleet after forty-seven days. Eustache Garnier becomes seigneur of the town.

1157. Severe damage inflicted on town and fortifications by an earthquake.

1187–92. Abandoned by the Franks after their defeat at Hattîn, the town is occupied by Saladin. Its defences are largely dismantled. In 1192 Saladin hands back part of Renaud de Sagette's estate, but no systematic rebuilding is undertaken at first.

1228–29. Şaidâ is finally restored to the Franks and re-fortified. Work begins on the sea-fort (Qal'at al-bahr).

1249–53. The town is briefly occupied by the Arabs and the residential quarter devastated yet again, though the new sea-fort apparently remains in Frankish hands.

1253–54. The town defences and citadel are rebuilt on a grand scale by King Louis IX of France under the local supervision of Simon de Montcéliart.

1260. Şaidâ is attacked and partially destroyed by the Mongols after disputes between Julien de Sagette, seigneur of the town, and the Mongol governor of Damascus. Together with the castle of Beaufort, the town is acquired by the Templars soon afterwards, and plays a minor part in the inter-Frankish conflicts of the late 13th century. The town is attacked by Bohemond VII of Antioch.

1291. After the fall of Acre, the Templars flee from there to Şaidâ, where they elect their new Grand Master. They fail to withstand the Arab onslaught, however, and escape by sea to Cyprus. The town falls after their departure and its fortifications are dismantled.

Late 16th and early 17th centuries. The town plays a major role in Levantine commerce and is re-fortified. Several large *hane* or warehouses are erected.

The general appearance of the town continued to undergo widespread changes in the centuries that followed, and the harbour fort suffered considerable damage during an Anglo-Austrian naval bombardment in 1840.

Bibliography:
Enc. Isl. IV, 434–35 (P. Schwarz 1934);
Enlart, *Monuments II*, 336–39;
Deschamps, *Châteaux II*, 224–233, containing exhaustive bibliographical references.

CHASTEL PELERIN   Plate 98

Frk. Chastel Pèlerin, Castel Pellegrino, etc.,
also castrum Filii Dei; Arab. 'Atlît.

Description

Ruined castle and town situated on a small rocky peninsula about ten miles south of the port of Haifa (Israel). The castle was guarded on the landward side by a deep fosse and a strong cross-wall with three stout towers built into it. The fortifications on the seaward side are more dilapidated and have not yet been excavated, but it is clear that behind the outer wall and intervening forecourt stood a donjon whose flanks were reinforced with projecting towers (like the donjon of the Templar fortress at Tortosa?), while stabling, living-quarters and magazines were located in the buildings which bordered the rocky shore. The urban area (approximately 600 yards long and 150–200 yards wide) has been only partly excavated (baths, church and stables). It was lightly fortified with a single wall.

History

1217–18. Gautier d'Avesnes builds a new castle with the aid of numerous pilgrims (hence its name) and several members of the Order of the Temple and Teutonic Order, to replace an older Templar castle (Le Destroit, Districtum, Petra Incisa, etc.) about a mile away. During its construction the knights excavated the foundations of walls which once belonged to a small Phoenician settlement, together with a cache of coins. Some of the masonry is re-used and the gold added to the building fund.

1219–20. While still under construction, the castle is subjected to a preliminary Arab attack. It is besieged the following year, but Malik al-Mu'aẓẓam's forces withdraw after a month without accomplishing anything.

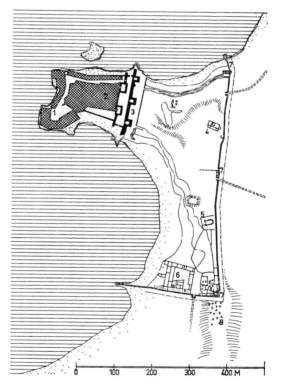

Plan 22: CHASTEL PELERIN – 'ATLIT
General ground-plan of settlement, scale 1:10,000. 1, Inner fortress. 2, Probable site of Great Donjon. 3, Wall and fosse. 4, Baths. 5, Ruined church. 6, Stables. 7, Town wall and fosse. 8, Phoenician burialground. (Based on results of excavation (1930–35) by C. N. Johns.)

1229. Visit of Emperor Frederick II, whose claims upon the castle are only dismissed after grave threats have been issued by the Order of the Temple.

1250–51. King Louis IX (Saint-Louis) lodges his wife, Marguerite de Provence, at the castle while living in Acre. His son Pierre is born there. The town church, of which little survives, was probably built about this time.

1265. The town is destroyed by the Arabs.

1291. The Franks are compelled to abandon the castle after the fall of Acre and withdraw to Cyprus. Chastel Pèlerin subsequently becomes a minor regional capital and is occupied by a small Mameluke garrison.

For a considerable period in the early 19th century, the castle served as a source of building materials for the defences of Acre, with the result that nearly all of it was demolished.

Bibliography:

Rey, *Arch. Militaire* 93–100 (incl. sketch-map);
Conder – Kitchener, *Survey I*, 293–300;
Enlart, *Monuments II*, 93–96;
Deschamps, *Châteaux I* (cf. Index) and II, 24–33, 237 et seq.;
C. N. Johns, *A Guide to Atlit*, Jerusalem 1947
C. N. Johns, 'Excavations at Pilgrims Castle ('Atlît)', in: *Quarterly Dept. Antiquit. Palestine I*, 1931, 111–129; 2, 1933, 41–104; 3, 1934, 137–164; 4, 1935, 122–165;
Fedden – Thomson, 41 et seq., 82–85.

ACRE-AKKON   Plates 99–100

Gr. Ptolemais; Frk. Saint-Jean d'Acre, Acri, etc.; Arab. 'Akkâ.

Description

Sea-port in the north of Israel, situated on a slightly projecting spit of land beside the Bay of Haifa. Although it was the Franks' chief harbour at the time of the Crusades, Acre has preserved very few relics of its Frankish prime. The only tokens of two centuries of Frankish rule are a few church or palace vaults and one of the towers which formed part of the city's defences.

History

636. A harbour which enjoyed considerable importance in the ancient world, Acre is captured and extensively rebuilt by the Arabs.

1099. The first Crusader army refrains from attacking Acre because its Fatimid emir promises to submit if Jerusalem falls.

1103–04. After an unsuccessful preliminary attack, the city is besieged by a Frankish army under King Baldwin I, supported by a Genoese fleet, and taken after twenty days.

1110. An Egyptian attempt at recapture is thwarted with the aid of a Norman fleet. Acre becomes the chief port of the Kingdom of Jerusalem and is directly subordinated to its rulers.

1187. Saladin captures the city without encountering serious resistance after his victory at Hattîn. The defences are strengthened. They consist, on the landward side, of a single wall and a fosse.

1189–91. The city is besieged, first by Guy of Lusignan and then (in 1191) by Richard Cœur de Lion and Philip of France. Acre is recaptured after a series of fierce assaults and succeeds Jerusalem as the residence of the Latin Patriarch and the Frankish kings. The dilapidated defences are repaired by Richard Cœur de Lion.

1202. The city is damaged by an earthquake.

1250–54. Improvements are made to the northern defences and the fortifications of the new suburb during the stay of King Louis IX (Saint-Louis). Acre has been the real capital of the kingdom for some time now. Representatives of almost all the important commercial powers (Genoa, Venice, Florence, Lucca, Pisa and others) live there in their own residential quarters; many have separate fortifications and defensible churches. The city is a hotbed of intrigue. Towards the end of the 13th century it contains about forty churches and numerous monasteries.

1263 and 1266. Sultan Baibars attacks the city without success.

1285. The fortifications in the north-east corner are strengthened by King Edward I of England and Countess Alice de Blois.

1291. The city is besieged by Sultan al-Malik al-Ašraf, who attacks it with mines and siege-engines. Acre falls after about six weeks. The military knights stubbornly defend their headquarters but are eventually forced to flee to Cyprus with the rest. The city is devastated.

After remaining in eclipse until the end of the 16th century, Acre was rebuilt by Emir Fahr ad-dîn and completely re-fortified in the late 18th century by the Turkish pasha Ahmed Cezzar, with the result that the old defences have disappeared. The city regained importance as a harbour during this period.

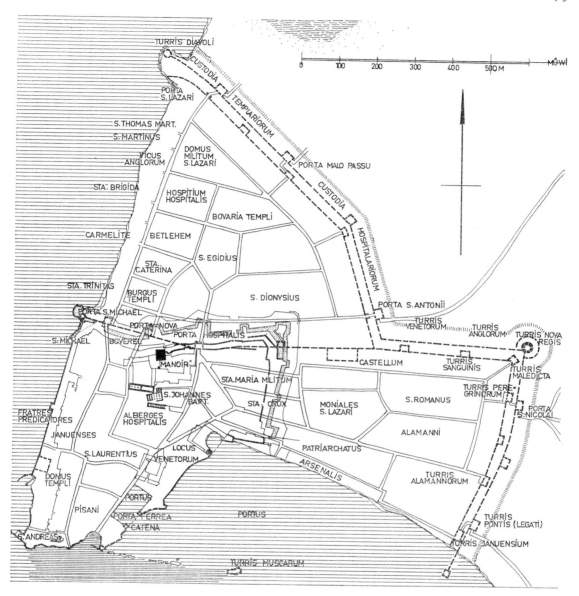

Plan 23: ACRE. *Town plan embodying attempted reconstruction of old walls, scale 1 : 10,000, based on the present-day town plan (modern fortifications indicated by broken lines) but showing quarters referred to in old maps of the 14th-18th centuries and giving their original Latin names. The lay-out of streets is based partly on these maps and partly on traces still discernible in the modern town. Extant or recently excavated buildings are reproduced in black (e. g., remnants of the Hospitaller quarter and the tower, or so-called Burğ es-Sulṭân, which still stands beside the harbour).*

Bibliography:
Enc. Isl. (2) I, 351–52 (Fr. Buhl 1960);
Rey, *Arch. Militaire*, 171 et seq.;
Rey, *Les colonies franques de Syrie au 12e et 13e siècles*, Paris 1883;
Rey, 'Etude sur la topographie de la ville d'Acre au XIIIe siècle', in: *Mém. Soc. Ant. de France*, Vol. 39, Paris 1879;
Conder-Kitchener, *Survey I*, 160–67;
Deschamps, *Châteaux I*, 65–69, containing old plan of city (1686);
N. Makhouly – C. N. Johns, *Guide to Acre*, Jerusalem 1946, with exhaustive descriptions, plans and bibliographical data.

CAESAREA   Plates 101–103

Gr. Kaisareia Stratonos; Lat. Caesarea maritima; Frk. Césarée, Sezare, Cezaire, Sezaire, Sessaire, etc.; Arab. Qaiṣariya, Qesari.

Description

Formerly an important ancient and medieval harbour in Palestine, situated in a natural bay formed by two rocky promontories between Haifa and Tel Aviv. The site, which remained deserted from the end of the Middle Ages until the late 19th century, when it became sparsely repopulated, has been undergoing excavation since 1958. Parts of the medieval fortifications have been unearthed, together with ancient and medieval buildings. The stoutly built defences enclosed an approximately trapezoid area beside the bay. They were adjoined in the south by the old citadel, which occupied the spit of land at the southern end of the harbour and was protected on the landward side by a strong wall.

History

639. Caesarea is captured by the Arabs and heavily fortified.

1101. After capturing Arsûf, King Baldwin I attacks Caesarea and takes it by storm after a brief siege. Its inhabitants are brutally massacred by the Frankish army.

1187. Saladin captures Caesarea after defeating the Franks at Hattîn and destroys the ancient fortifications.

1191. The deserted town is occupied by Franks under the command of Richard Cœur de Lion. It is rebuilt and its defences restored.

1218. A new castle is erected by Gautier d'Avesnes and Jean de Brienne.

1220. Caesarea falls to the army of Sultan al-Malik al-Muʿaẓẓam because of negligence on the part of the garrison.

1251–52. The town's defences are considerably improved after its recapture. These improvements include additions to the gatehouse and the laying of a large revetted fosse and continuous talus.

1265. Caesarea surrenders to Sultan Baibars' army after a siege of only seven days, though the citadel holds out somewhat longer. The town is subjected to systematic destruction after its capture.

1291. Devastated yet again during the reign of Sultan al-Ašraf so as to deprive the Franks of a potential bridge-head, Caesarea thereafter remains deserted.

Bibliography:
Enc. Isl. II, 707–08 (M. Streck 1927);
Conder – Kitchener, *Survey II*, 13–29;
Enlart, *Monuments II*, 85–89;
Illustrated London News, Vol. 243, Nos. 6482–83 (field report).

MONTFORT   Plates 104–105

Frk. Frans Chastiau; Ger. Starkenberg, Starkenburg; Arab. Qalʿat Qourein.

Description

Ruined castle in northern Israel, about twenty-two miles north of Haifa, situated on a steep ridge in the outlying spurs of the mountain range north-west of Lake Tiberias. The badly dilapidated stronghold was separated from the mountain by a wide fosse and reinforced on the same flank by a donjon (probably semicircular). The site is narrow, elongated and asymmetrical, and the separate constituents of the castle are densely concentrated. The slope on the northern flank is occupied by a rather more spacious lower fortress.

History

1227–29. Jacques de Armigdala, Seigneur de Mande-lée, relinquishes the castle to the Teutonic Knights, who convert it into a repository for the archives and treasury of their Order (1229). This reconstruction work is sanctioned by the treaty between Emperor Frederick II and Sultan Malik al-Kâmil, and supervised by Grand Master Hermann von Salza.

1230. Pope Gregory IV dispatches a papal letter designed to assist the Order in rebuilding the castle.

1266. Sultan Baibars besieges Montfort but is repulsed.

1271. Besieged for a second time, the castle surrenders to Baibars after being attacked with siege-engines and extensively undermined. The Knights withdraw to Acre. The castle is dismantled and abandoned for good.

Bibliography:
Rey, *Arch. Militaire 142–151 and Plan 15;*
Conder-Kitchener, *Survey I 186–190;*
Deschamps, *Châteaux II 139 ff.;*
Bashford Dean, 'The exploration of a Crusaders fortress (Montfort) in Palestine.' *In: Bull. Metrop. Museum New York Nr. 22 (1927).*

TOPRAKKALE   Plates 106–108

Gr. name uncertain, perh. Epiphanias; Frk. Tilium; Arab Tell Hamdûn, Thil, Til, etc.; Turk. Toprakkale.

Description

Castle and village on the eastern edge of the broad plain of Adana in Southern Turkey, situated in a commanding position in the rolling hill-country adjoining the western slopes of the Amanus range. The castle stands on a rocky outcrop which has been artificially augmented by the debris of an ancient settlement, and is comparatively well preserved. It consists of a spacious but lightly fortified lower fortress, and, higher to the east, an upper fortress which is cut off from the former by a cross-wall reinforced with four strong towers. Steep rocky slopes afford excellent natural protection to its other three flanks, which are guarded by an outer wall incorporating semicircular towers and continuous defensive galleries. In the south-west corner of the inner ward and abutting on the south-west corner-tower stands a palatial hall. Vaulted magazines, stables and simple offices of a like nature run along the entire length of the west wall, but there are two larger and more elaborate chambers in the north-west corner. Apart from two cisterns, no architectural relics survive in the interior of the spacious courtyard, although smaller buildings must have stood there at one time.

History

It is probable that the castle had long been in existence and played a prominent role during the Byzantine emperors' campaigns in Northern Syria in the latter half of the 10th century, but its Greek name has yet to be identified and no details of its previous history can therefore be ascertained.

1137. The castle is first referred to by its accepted Frankish name in connection with the near-destruction of the Kingdom of Lesser Armenia by Emperor John II Comnenus (1118–43).

1151. The Armenians capture the castle from the Byzantines.

1154. Attacked by the Seljuks at the instigation of the Byzantine Emperor, the castle is relieved only with the aid of Franks from Bağras.

1158. Toprakkale is captured by Emperor Manuel Comnenus (1143–80) but probably recaptured shortly afterwards by the Armenians.

1185. The Armenians cede Toprakkale to Antioch as ransom for Prince Ruben, captured by Bohemond III.

1194. The castle is restored to the Armenians. Willebrand of Oldenburg (1211) records that it was already heavily fortified at this juncture. It continues to play an important role in the subsequent conflicts between the princes of Antioch and the Armenian kings.

Late 13th century (perhaps 1293). The castle is devastated by Maleluke forces campaigning against the Armenians, and is never properly rebuilt. It changes

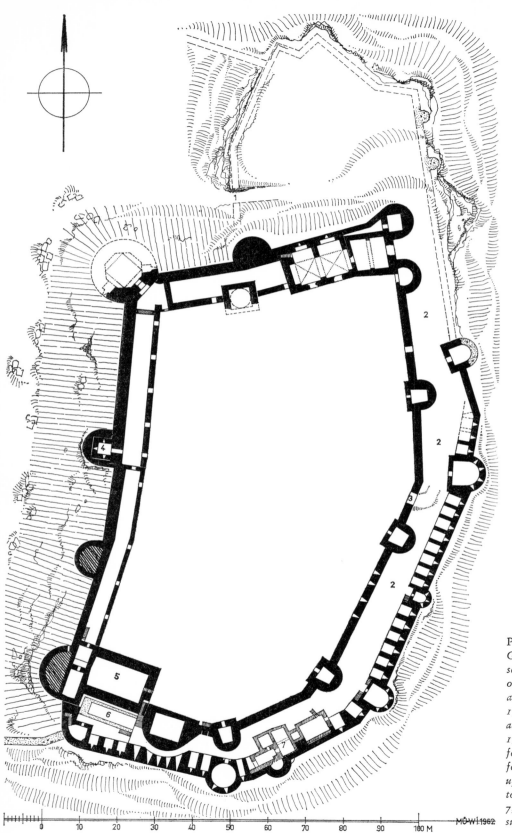

Plan 24: TOPRAKKALE.
Ground-plan of upper fortress,
scale 1:1000. Buildings
of the Byzantine, Frankish
and Armenian periods in black,
15th- and 16th-century
additions finely hatched.
1, Main access from lower
fortress. 2, Forecourt of upper
fortress. 3, Main gate of
upper fortress. 4, Byzantine
tower. 5, Great Hall. 6, Cistern.
7, Baths. (Based on author's
survey.)

hands several times thereafter, but remains in Mameluke possession from 1337 until captured by the Ottoman Sultans in 1491, when it ceases to have any further importance.

Bibliography:
J. Gottwald, 'Die Burg Til im südöstlichen Kilikien', in: *Byzant. Zeitschr.* 40, 1940, 89–104.

SIS (KOZAN)   Plate 109

Gr. Sision Kastron; Arab. Sîsiya, Ḥiṣn Sîsiya;
Frk. – Lat. Sis, Sisia, Assis, Oussis, etc.;
modern Turk. name Kozan.

Description

Castle and town in Southern Turkey, about forty miles north-east of Adana, commanding a road which leads down from the Taurus into the broad plains below. The residential quarter is laid out in terraces on the slopes beneath the castle, while the castle itself extends for roughly 1000 yards along the narrow ridge above. The main fortifications and royal residence are situated at the southern extremity of this ridge. The whole fortress evolved from the rocky terrain on which it stands, and displays the features usually associated with Armenian castles, namely, semicircular towers and neatly dressed bossed stonework. The residential quarter was never fortified.

History

The town played a major role in the Byzantine-Arab border disputes of the 8th-9th centuries, first as a Byzantine and then as an Arab frontier fortress.

Early 13th century. Having briefly been a royal seat in the early days of Lesser Armenia, the town is made a seat of government by King Leo II and considerably enlarged. The defences of the upper fortress date from this period.

1266. After defeating the Armenians at Darbsâk, a Mameluke army advances on Sis and devastates the town, burning the cathedral and despoiling the royal tombs.

1274–75. The town is again sacked by one of Sultan Baibars' Mameluke armies, but the citadel holds out.

1292. The Armenian Patriarch settles in Sis after escaping from Rum Kale.

Sis becomes the target of numerous Mameluke raids in the decades that follow (1298, 1303, 1321, 1339, 1359, 1369), but, although the town suffers each time, the high-lying citadel withstands attack. Several councils are held at Sis to discuss the problem of Church Union (1307, 1309 and 1342).

1374–75. After a protracted siege, the citadel falls into Mameluke hands as a result of treachery. The last Armenian king, Leo VI, is taken prisoner and borne off to Cairo.

The town remained the seat of the Armenian Catholicos until the 19th century, but has no other claims to importance.

Bibliography:
Enc. Isl. IV, 487–89 (V. F. Büchner 1934);
Fedden – Thomson, 89–94.

YILAN KALESI   Plate 110

(Ancient and medieval designations still unidentified)

Description

Castle in Southern Turkey, situated near the Ceyhan river on a precipitous ridge between Ceyhan and Misis. The fact that it commands an excellent view of the entire Adana plain and is in visual contact with a whole series of neighbouring castles must have made it one of the most important strongholds in the Kingdom of Lesser Armenia.

Yilan Kalesi evolved naturally from the rocky terrain. It consists of an upper fortress guarded by seven stout semicircular towers and a small outer fortress which juts southwards. At the foot of the eastern slope stands an outer wall reinforced with bastions. Although well-preserved, the castle has still to be investigated and accurately surveyed.

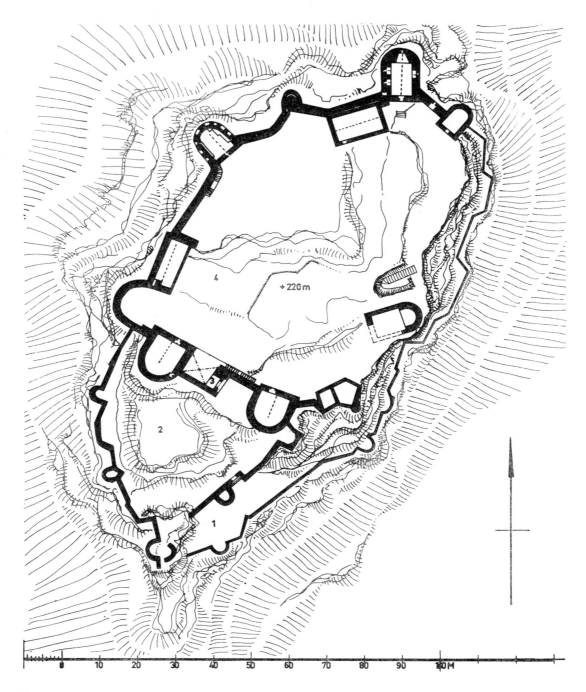

Plan 25:   YILAN KALESI. *Ground-plan of castle, scale 1:1000. 1, Forecourt. 2, Outer fortress. 3, Main gate of upper fortress. 4, Inner bailey of upper fortress. (Based on a survey by K. Bockmann.)*

History

Since the castle's ancient and medieval names are unknown, no details of its history have yet been ascertained. To judge by individual features, however, it should be attributed to the reign of King Leo II.

The subsequent history of the place probably resembles that of near-by Toprakkale. It is unlikely that either castle fulfilled any major function after the country had been conquered by the Ottomans.

Bibliography:
J. Gottwald, 'Burgen und Kirchen im mittleren Kilikien', in: *Byzant. Zeitschr.* 41, 1941, 82–93 (containing false attribution).
G. R. Youngs, 'Three Cilician castles', in: *Anatol. Stud.* 15, 1965, 125 et seq.

CORYCUS
Plates 111–114

Gr. Korykos; Frk. Korghos, Curco, Culchus, Curchus, etc.; Turk. Korgos, Korikos.

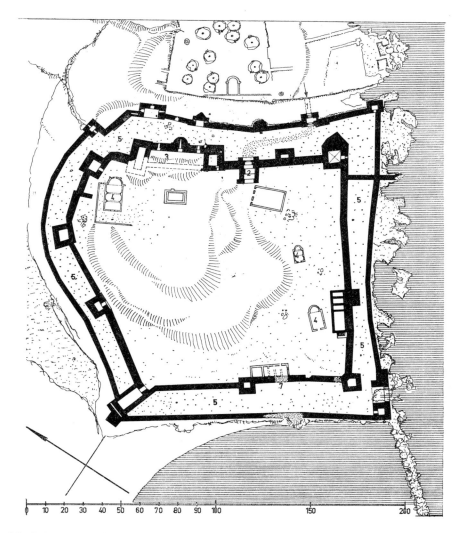

Plan 26: CORYCUS *Ground-plan of mainland castle, scale 1:2000. 1, Former drawbridge and outer gate. 2, Inner gate. 3, Ruins of Great Hall. 4, Chapels. 5, Forecourt. 6, Mole. 7, Ruins of Roman gate, incorporated in the medieval castle. (Based on Herzfeld-Guyer.)*

Description

Castle between Mersin and Silifke in Southern Turkey, on the site of a harbour town which enjoyed some importance in the ancient world. Situated to the west of the ancient residential quarter and adjacent to the ancient harbour, which was well protected by a mole built of massive pieces of rock, the castle was designed to guard the harbour in conjunction with the outlying island fort.

This small island fort consists of a single polygonal wall reinforced with semicircular and rectangular towers, and has a cistern and small chapel in its inner courtyard. The mainland castle, which is larger and more heavily fortified, consists of two concentric curtain walls of asymmetrical design, the outer ring being reinforced by small isolated bastions and a fosse. The inner ring is guarded by twelve strong towers of varying shape. The three towers in the north-east corner are symmetrically arranged and clearly formed part of a sizeable hall. There are numerous smaller structures in the castle's interior (chapels, cisterns, etc.).

History

1100–4. The island fort is presumed to have been founded during an expedition against the Armenians led by the Byzantine admiral Eustathius, probably with the aim of dominating the town and harbour without having to occupy the mainland.

Late 12th – early 13th centuries. The Armenians gain possession of the whole site. Corycus is not only a stronghold on the frontiers of the Western world but an important harbour where residencies are maintained by the Italian naval powers. The town is initially owned, and its defences rebuilt, by the Armenian crown.

Mid-13th century. Oschîn, a member of the royal family, becomes lord of Corycus.

1361. After the collapse of the Kingdom of Lesser Armenia, the town's inhabitants request the kings of Cyprus for aid in repelling incessant attacks by the Karaman Turks. Robert of Lusignan lands and restores the fortifications.

1367. The town is again besieged by the Turks.

Mid-15th century. The castle is captured from the Lusignans by the Karamanoğlu, allegedly as a result of treachery. It does not remain in the hands of its new masters for long. Having been an object of strife since 1471, it is acquired by the Ottomans in 1482, upon the death of the last Karamanoğlu prince.

The harbour continued to play a subordinate role until the advent of modern times, but the town later fell into decay.

Bibliography:
E. Herzfeld – S. Guyer, *Monumenta Asiae Minoris Antiqua*, Vol. II: *Meriamlik und Korykos, zwei christliche Ruinenstätten des Rauhen Kilikien*, Manchester 1930, containing full bibliographical data.

SILIFKE   Plates 115–116

Anc. Seleukeia, Seleucia Trachaea, Seleucia Ciliciae, etc.; Frk. Selef; Turk. Silifke.

Description

Castle and small country town in Southern Turkey, roughly ten miles from the estuary of the Gök-Su (anc. Calycadnus) in the outlying spurs of the Taurus Mountains. The castle evolved wholly from the terrain, being built on a rocky mound whose moderately steep flanks fall away evenly all round. It is more or less oval in shape, and surrounding it is a simple polygonal perimeter wall guarded by several stout semicircular towers and reinforced in places by an outer wall. A broad fosse was hewn out of the solid rock at various points.

Although the castle's outer walls are fairly well preserved, virtually nothing remains of the interior.

History

8th – 10th centuries. A fortified settlement of long standing, Silifke plays an important part in the frontier wars between Byzantium and the Arabs.

c. 1098. It is occupied by the Franks at some unspecified date during the First Crusade and annexed to the Principality of Antioch.

1104. The Byzantines take advantage of Frankish weakness after Bohemond's severe defeat at Harrân to recapture the place. Like those of Corycus, Silifke's defences are subsequently rebuilt by the Byzantine Admiral Eustathius. The castle above the town should probably be attributed to this period as well.

Early 12th century. Silifke is presumed to have changed hands several times in the course of fighting between Byzantium and Lesser Armenia during the first half of the 12th century, and is not firmly in Armenian hands until its end.

1190. Emperor Frederick I (Barbarossa), while on the Third Crusade, is drowned in the neighbourhood of Silifke while crossing the Calycadnus.

1210–26. King Leo II of Armenia cedes the town to the Hospitallers in exchange for the services of four hundred heavily-armed knights. To avoid becoming entangled in Armenian internal disputes (Princess Isabel flees to Silifke before her marriage to the future King Hethum I), the knights sell the town to its Armenian besiegers. An inscription records that the new king subsequently improved the castle.

It is probable that Silifke continued to belong to the Kingdom of Lesser Armenia until the latter's downfall. During the 15th century it played a part in the disputes between the Ottoman sultan Mehmet II and local Karamanoğlu rulers, who were backed by Venice, but was firmly held by the Ottomans after their victory. The castle was severely damaged by a gun-powder explosion during the latter fighting.

Bibliography:
Enc. Isl. IV, 228 et seq. (Cl. Huart 1934);
J. Keil – A. Wilhelm, *Denkmäler aus dem Rauhen Kilikien (Monumenta Asiae Minoris Antiqua, Vol. III),* Manchester 1931;
Fedden – Thomson, 94–7.

ANAMUR
Plate 117

Gr. Anemourion; Frk. Stallimuri, Stalemura, etc.; Turk. Anamur, Mamuriye, Mamur Kalesi.

Description

Village and castle on the southern coast of Turkey, situated near the mouth of a small river and a headland of the same name. The large, stoutly constructed castle incorporates thirty-six towers and consists of three baileys separated by walls fortified with towers. The inner fortress proper stands on a small rocky mound immediately beside the sea. Extending to the north and east of it are two spacious baileys, the latter facing the sea and the inner, northern bailey being protected on the landward flank by a fosse and a particularly strong wall. Still in an excellent state of preservation thanks to restoration work carried out in the 19th century, Anamur was one of the most powerful strongholds in the Kingdom of Lesser Armenia.

History

The castle was erected on the site of an ancient settlement, probably by the Armenians. It is presumed to have been in the possession of the Frankish kings of Cyprus for some time after the Kingdom of Lesser Armenia ceased to exist, but subsequently fell into Seljuk hands.

1373. Now held by the Karamanoğlu, the castle is badly damaged during an attack by the Cypriot fleet under Jean de Tyr.

1469–70. Anamur is restored by the Ottomans.

1840. Repairs are carried out on the castle, which is still occupied by a small garrison. The small mosque and minaret in the inner bailey are built at the same time. Further repairs are undertaken towards the end of the century, but discontinued after the collapse of the large corner-tower in the inner fortress.

Bibliography:
Pauly – Wissowa, *Realencyclopädie II, 2182* (Hirschfeld 1894);
Enc. Isl. (2) I, 495 (Fr. Taeschner 1960);
L. de Mas-Latrie, *L'Ile de Chypre. Sa situation présente et ses souvenirs du moyen-âge,* Paris 1879, 231 et seq., 261 et seq.;
Fedden – Thomson, 97–8.

BODONITSA
Plate 118

Frk. Medietas Bondonicie, Boudonitza.

Description

Castle in the eastern part of Central Greece, situated in the highlands north of the Mavropotamos (the Cephissus of ancient Boeotia) and guarding the southern approaches of Thermopylae. Both the castle and the small town which once adjoined it are severely dilapidated. Remnants of the outer walls and a stoutly built tower of squarish proportions are all that survives of the castle itself.

History

1205. During the campaigns waged in Central and Southern Greece by Boniface of Montferrat, King of Salonica, the district south of Thermopylae is given in fee to Count Guido Pallavicini, a member of his army. (Guido Pallavicini, whose family came from the region of Parma, was known among the Greeks as Marchesopoulos. He remained a prominent member of the petty kingdom's nobility until its downfall.)

1225–26. In company with the Duchy of Athens, Bodonitsa remains Frankish after the collapse of the Kingdom of Salonica. On the instructions of Pope Honorius III, the small castle's defences are put in order and money collected for their further improvement.

c. 1252. Bodonitsa is attacked by the Greeks, presumably as part of the campaign waged against Michael II of Epirus by Emperor John III Vatatzes (1222–54). The Greeks are repelled by Guillaume de Villehardouin.

Early 14th century. After the death of the third and last seigneur of Bodonitsa during the savage battle at Lake Copais in 1311, the County is divided between the widow of Alberto Pallavicini and his daughter Guglielma. It later passes in its entirety to Francesco Giorgio, Guglielma's son by Niccolo Giorgio, whose successors continue to rule the County under the suzerainty of the Catalonian rulers of Athens. The family remains Venetian, however.

1410. The castle is stormed by the Ottoman sultan Musa. After its capture, Niccolo II Giorgio is carried off to Edirne as a prisoner but later released.

1414. On 20 June, Bodonitsa is again captured by the Turks, who inflict damage on the town and castle. Niccolo flees to Venice. His domain is restored to him by the peace treaty of 1416, but he declines to accept it.

The place remains under Turkish rule and falls into decline.

Bibliography:

G. Schlumberger, *Numismatique de l'Orient Latin*, Paris 1878, 350–1;

W. Miller, *The Latins in the Levant. A history of Frankish Greece*, London 1908, pass.;

J. Longnon, *L'Empire Latin de Constantinople et la Principauté de Morée*, Paris 1949, pass.

CASTEL TORNESE
Plates 119–120

Frk. Clairmont, Clermont; Gr. Chlemutzi.

Description

Castle in the north-west of the Peloponnese, about three miles from the sea. Situated on a flat hill-top on the rocky promontory of Chlemutzi, it has a commanding view of the interior as well as the straits between the mainland and the off-shore island of Zakinthos. The small township of Clarentza served the castle as a harbour.

The castle consists of an irregular hexagonal inner fortress, a sort of donjon with a small open courtyard and barrel-vaulted chambers running round the interior, and another expanse of open courtyard adjoining it in the west. Disregarding minor alterations, the whole building has survived in its original state. The structural technique is generally Byzantine, but strong West European influence is detectable in individual features.

History

1220–3. Geoffroy I Villehardouin erects the castle while feuding with the clergy of Achaea. Later on, with the permission of King Louis IX, he builds a mint there which produces replicas of 'Tournois', or coins struck at Tours in France (hence the name).

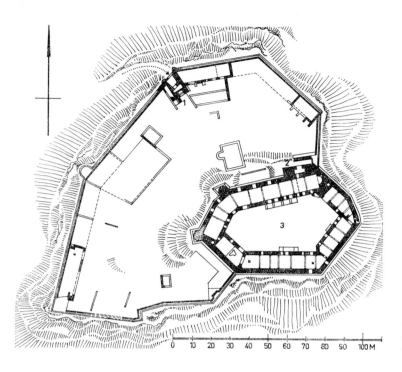

Plan 27: CASTEL TOR-
NESE – CHLEMUTZI.
*Ground-plan of castle, scale
1:2000. I, Main gate of outer
fortress. 2, Gate of inner
fortress. 3, Inner fortress.
(Based on Sotiriou.)*

1313–16. The castle changes hands repeatedly in the course of disputes between Ferdinand of Majorca and Louis of Burgundy over who should succeed to the Principality of Achaea. It remains in Burgundian hands until the early 15th century, when it is regained by the Byzantines.

c. 1480. Castel Tornese is acquired by the Turks but changes hands between Venice and Turkey several times during its subsequent career. Having forfeited its strategic importance, the castle is left in its medieval state.

Bibliography:
R. Traquair, 'Mediaeval fortresses in N. W. Peloponnesos', in: *Ann. Brit. School Athens 13*, 1907, 272 et seq.;
Georgios Sotiriou, 'Le Château de Chlemoutzi et son atelier monétaire', in: *Journ. Intern. d'archéol. numismat. 19*, 1918–19, 276;
Kevin Andrews, *Castles of the Morea*, Princeton 1953, 146–158.

NAVARINO

Plates 121–122

*Frk. Chastel du Port de Junch; It. Zunchio;
Gr. Palaia Avarino, after the Byzantine name of the castle.*

Description

Castle on the south-west coast of the Peloponnese, situated on a precipitous massif north of the modern township of Pylos (New Navarino), high above the bay of the same name. It is connected to the mainland by two narrow causeways and separated from the rocky island of Sphakteria by a narrow channel.

The lay-out of the castle was determined by the nature of its site. It is divided into an upper and lower fortress by an interior wall, but neither half contains any relics of the Frankish era.

History

c. 1278. Nicolas de St Omer erects the castle for his nephew Nicolas III on the site of an earlier Byzantine fortress which, in its turn, occupied the site of the ancient town of Koryphasion. Many relics of the fortifications and buildings of the ancient town can be seen in the vicinity of the castle, and stones from the former were undoubtedly used in the construction of the latter.

Early 14th century. The castle falls briefly into the hands of the Genoese, who use it as a base for attacks on Venetian strongholds in Messenia.

1366. Marie de Bourbon, widow of the Prince of Achaea, defends the castle against the combined forces of the Frankish barons and the Archbishop of Patras.

1381. The castle is captured by the Grand Company of Navarre, a body of Spanish mercenaries which rapidly gains control of Frankish Morea.

1423. Venice acquires Navarino from its last seigneur, Centurione Zaccaria. It remains a Venetian possession after the Turkish conquest of Morea and is not captured by Sultan Bâyezid II until 1500. The castle changes hands repeatedly and its fortifications are substantially altered during the wars of the 17th-18th centuries.

Bibliography:
Kevin Andrews, *Castles of the Morea,* Princeton 1953, 40–8 and plans;
Guide Bleu, Grèce, Paris 1956, 401–4.

MISTRA   Plates 123–124

Description

Ruined castle and town near Sparta, situated on the eastern slopes of the Taygetos Mountains about three miles from the river Evrotas. The castle occupies an almost impregnable position on a ridge which falls away steeply on all sides, while the town is built in terraces on the equally steep north-east and east slopes.

The castle's elongated shape was determined by the mountainous terrain. The lower fortress (*c.* 1935 feet above sea level) takes up most of the ridge. North of it and somewhat higher (2036 feet at its highest point) stands the upper fortress, whose donjon faces the lower fortress in the normal way. Access is from the north, via steep and winding mountain paths.

The small town was enclosed by two separate perimeter walls, an upper ring surrounding the main residential quarter and the despot's palace on its projecting terrace in the north, and a lower ring embracing the sparsely inhabited lower part of the town and several monasteries.

History

Mid-13th century. The castle and settlement are founded by Guillaume de Villehardouin when the Frankish conquest of the Peloponnese is almost complete.

1259–62. After being defeated as a result of treachery by Emperor Michael VIII Palaeologus of Byzantium, who holds him captive for three years, Guillaume de Villehardouin is compelled to surrender Mistra and other places as ransom.

1262–1460. Mistra continues to be ruled by the various Byzantine despots of Morea, who manage to remain semi-independent of the imperial court at Constantinople.

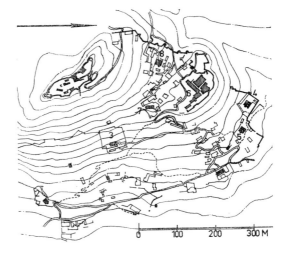

Plan 28: MISTRA. *Town plan, scale 1:10,000. 1, Castle of Guillaume de Villehardouin. 2, Peribleptos Monastery. 3, Pantanassa Monastery. 4, Church and Monastery of the Hodigitria (Aphentiko). 5, Church of St Theodore. 6, Palace of the Byzantine despots. 7, Monemvasia Gate and Church of St Nicholas. 8, Church of St Sophia. (Based on Hadzidakis.)*

1460. The town falls into the hands of the Turks and remains under their control, with brief intermissions in 1464 and 1687, until the end of Turkish domination.

1770. The town is devastated by fire. Apart from the castle itself, no relics of the brief period of Frankish occupation have survived there.

Bibliography:
Kevin Andrews, *Castles of the Morea*, Princeton 1953, 159–182;
M. Hadzidakis, *Mystras*, Athens 1948.

nese. It remains under the suzerainty of the despots until the Turks conquer the country in 1460.

1821. Theodoros Kolokotronis withdraws to Karytaina and improves the castle's defences.

Bibliography:
R. Traquair, 'Mediaeval fortresses in N. W. Peloponnesos', in: *Ann. Brit. School Athens 13*, 1907, 268 et seq.;
Guide Bleu: Grèce, Paris 1956, 468.

KARYTAINA

Plate 125

KANTARA

Plates 126–128

Frk. Le Candare, Le Candaire, La Candare, Kantara.

Description

Castle and village on the upper reaches of the river Alpheios in the Central Peloponnese. The castle stands on the summit of a steep crag beside a bend in the river, with the small settlement on a series of terraces below it.

The castle's elongated polygonal lay-out was dictated by the rocky terrain. Projecting to the east of it is a small outer fortress with the diminutive chapel of St Andrew nestling against the rock inside. In the cramped courtyard on the plateau are the remains of a hall and some vaulted cisterns. As a whole, the castle dates from the Frankish period, but it underwent minor alterations during the Greek war of independence.

Description

Castle on the northern coast of Cyprus, some 38 miles east of Kyrenia, situated about 2200 feet up on a steep ridge in the northern range. It is in visual contact with Buffavento and Famagusta. The wall which skirted the irregular perimeter of the precipitous site was reinforced with several strong towers and bastions, but only on the south and south-east flanks. Kantara is approached from the south by a mountain path which leads through a forecourt guarded by semicircular side-bastions. One unusual feature of the castle, which is in a fair state of preservation, is that the highest point in the interior is occupied by a small watch-tower.

History

1254. The castle is erected by Hugues de Bruyères, who has made Karytaina his main residence since the Frankish conquest of the Peloponnese. Hugues and his son Geoffroy are among the leading seigneurs of Frankish Morea, but their male line becomes extinct in 1272. The castle then passes to the Brienne family.

1320. Together with large tracts of Arcadia, the castle is recaptured for Byzantium by Andronicus Asan, one of the Byzantine rulers of the Pelopon-

History

1228–9. Cypriot troops under Anseau de Brie besiege the castle, which is occupied by supporters of Emperor Frederick II. They demolish a section of wall with a trabuch, or catapult, but the castle holds out until a skilful archer begins to pick off the defenders from a neighbouring rock.

1232. The castle is again occupied by loyalists but speedily recaptured by King Henry.

1373. After the occupation of Famagusta by the Genoese, Kantara becomes an important base from

which their activities can be kept under surveillance.
It continues to fulfill this function for some decades.

1391. King James I makes extensive additions
to Kantara and the castle of Sigouri for the above
purpose. In its present state, Kantara dates largely
from this period.

1525. The Venetian governors decide to dismantle
the now obsolete castle to save maintenance costs.
It has never been used since.

Bibliography:
Enlart, *Art Gothique II*, 648–654.

ST HILARION   Plates 129–132

Gr. Didymos, hence Frk. Dieudamour, Deudamor,
Dieu d'Amour, etc.; also St Hilarion, the form in
current use.

Description

Castle on the northern coast of Cyprus, immediately
south-west of Kyrenia. It lies at between 2300 and
2400 feet and commands the road between Kyrenia and Nicosia. Like the other mountain strong-

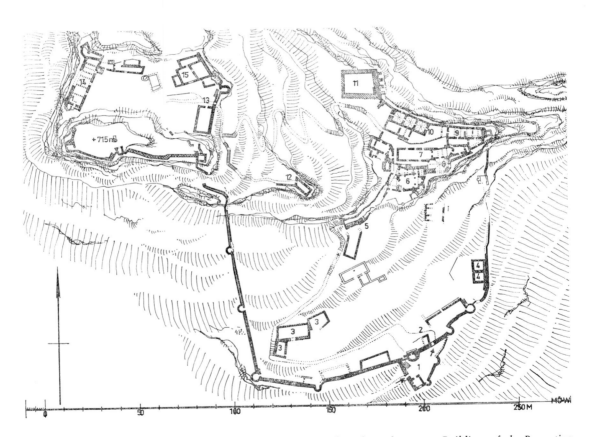

Plan 29:   ST HILARION-DIEUDAMOUR. *General-plan of castle, scale 1:2000. Buildings of the Byzantine*
period (10th century) in black, early Frankish additions cross-hatched, 14th-century buildings hatched. 1, Bar-
bican and outer gate. 2, Inner gate to lower bailey. 3, Stables. 4, Cisterns. 5, Inner gate to middle bailey.
6, Byzantine chapel (2nd half of 10th century). 7, Large hall (14th-century, on Byzantine foundations).
8, Belvedere. 9, Four-storeyed living-quarters. 10, Living-quarters (barracks?). 11, Cistern. 12, Prince
John's Tower. 13, Gate to upper bailey. 14, Royal apartments. 15, Offices and kitchens. (Based on A. H.
S. Megaw.)

holds of Cyprus, it evolved from the local topography, and consisted of a spacious outer fortress containing isolated buildings, a close-packed lower ward with a church, living-quarters and a large open cistern, and an upper fortress which housed the royal apartments and was separated from the lower fortress by a wall reinforced with towers.

History

Late 11th century (?). The castle is built, possibly in connection with an expedition by Emperor Alexius I (1081–1118) against the rebellious governor Rhapsomathes, as a safeguard against naval attack. Legend has it that the site was previously occupied by a monastery.

1229–30. Having recently been improved by the regent Jean d'Ibelin, St Hilarion falls into the hands of supporters of Emperor Frederick II and is taken only after a siege lasting nine months.

In the heyday of the Kingdom of Cyprus, the castle is used as a summer residence by the royal family.

1373. After capturing Famagusta, the Genoese try to invest Kyrenia as well. St Hilarion plays an important part in resisting the besiegers.

Early 16th century. St Hilarion and other mountain fortresses are dismantled by the Venetians to save maintenance costs.

Bibliography:

Enlart, *Art Gothique II*, 578–596;
Fedden – Thomson, 105 et seq.
A. H. S. Megaw, *A brief history and description of St Hilarion Castle.* Nicosia 1954

KYRENIA   Plates 133–136

Gr. Keryneia, Kerynia, Kyrene, etc;
Lat. Cyrinia;
Frk. Cerina, Cérines, Schernis, Ceraunie, etc.

Description

Small harbour town and important fortress on the northern coast of Cyprus. The external appearance of the large semi-rectangular citadel, with its massive rondels, large polygonal bastion in the south-

west, and thick curtain-walls, was largely determined by the Venetian phase of construction. The semicircular tower in the north-east corner and the adjoining curtain-walls, as well as considerable portions of the living-quarters and magazines bordering the spacious inner courtyard, date from the Frankish period. Relics of the Byzantine phase have survived only in a few of the interior walls and in the small chapel which was overlaid by the Venetian rondel in the north-west.

The remains of two semicircular towers are all that still exist of the original town defences.

History

1092. The town, originally founded in ancient times, is occupied by the Byzantine fleet during the campaign conducted against the rebellious governor Rhapsomathes by Emperor Alexius I (1081–1118).

1191. The Byzantine governor of Cyprus, Isaac Comnenus, plans to seek refuge at Kyrenia but is made prisoner before he can reach there. Kyrenia is besieged and captured by the Franks.

1211. The town's defences are still unimproved at the time of Willebrand von Oldenburg's visit, but the castle is evidently strengthened soon afterwards.

1228–34. The castle undergoes two sieges. It is captured by Emperor Frederick II's forces in 1232, after being invested for almost a year, but soon has to be restored to its Cypriot seigneurs.

14th century. The citadel functions as a State prison.

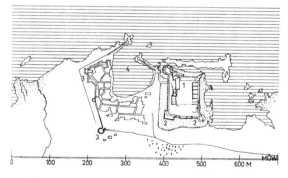

Plan 30: KYRENIA. *Town plan (as at end of 19th century), scale 1:10,000. Fortifications dating from the Byzantine and Frankish periods in black, buildings of the Venetian period unshaded. 1, Byzantine-Frankish citadel. 2, Bastions of the 15th–16th centuries. 3, Demolished sections of the town wall. 4, Harbour. (Based on Enlart.)*

1374. Kyrenia is besieged by Genoese from Famagusta, but King James I holds the castle in the face of bombardment by heavy stone cannon. St Hilarion plays a vital part in securing the defenders' rear.

1426. The Regent, Cardinal de Lusignan, withdraws to Kyrenia after being defeated at Khirokitia, but the Mamelukes refrain from testing the strength of its defences.

1460–3. As a result of a dispute over the right of succession between Charlotte de Lusignan and her bastard half-brother James II, Kyrenia is besieged for about three years. The governor, Sor de Naves, ultimately surrenders.

1544. The now obsolete fortress is extensively rebuilt by its new Venetian masters, who reinforce the south and west curtains and construct the rondel and large bastion.

1565. Despite these improvements, the Provveditore Ascanio Savorgnano pronounces the fortress in its present state to be too weak and unfavourably sited.

1570. The Turks capture Kyrenia without a fight. Under Turkish rule, the castle continues to be used as a garrison base and prison.

Bibliography:
Pauly – Wissowa, *Realencyclopädie Vol. XI*, 344–7 (Oberhummer 1921);
Enlart, *Art Gothique II, 559–578*;
Jeffery, *Historic Monuments of Cyprus,* Nicosia 1918, 304 et seq.;
A. H. S. Megaw in: *Report of the Department of Antiquities of Cyprus* 1936, 105–7.

BELLAPAIS   Plates 137–138

Frk. Lapaïs, Bellapais, also Abbaye de Episcopie, Episkopia.

Description

Premonstratensian monastery and village in the north of Cyprus, situated in the mountains a few miles south-east of Kyrenia. The monastery, which is extremely well preserved, follows the usual pattern. The open courtyard in the interior is lined with cloisters. In the south stands the small church, with a nave and two aisles, in the north the large refectory, and in the west the cellarium and kitchen, which has a small separate yard of its own.

History

Late 12th century. When Jerusalem fell in 1187, the monks there fled to Cyprus. Probably founded by Amalric of Lusignan (King of Jerusalem 1198–1205), the monastery of Bellapais was entrusted to a group of Augustins.

Early 13th century. Under the second Latin archbishop of Nicosia, Thierry, Bellapais adopted the Premonstratensian Rules. It grew considerably in the years that followed, notably during the reign of King Hugh III (1267–84), which probably witnessed the completion of the church. Hugh's two successors also fostered the monastery's expansion by adding to it and making bequests.

1373. The fortunes of the monastery were adversely affected by the fighting that broke out between the Cypriots and Genoese after the latter had captured Famagusta. It suffered particularly from the siege of Kyrenia.

Mid-16th century. The monastery deteriorated badly under Venetian rule. A thorough investigation was decreed in response to complaints from Provveditore Bernardo Sagredo (1562–4), but the monks were expelled by the Turks before any reforms could be instituted.

1570. After the Turkish conquest of Cyprus the monastery and its estates passed into Turkish ownership, though the villagers continued to use the church.

Bibliography:
Enlart, *Art Gothique I, 202–236.*

FAMAGUSTA   Plates 139–142

Gr. Ammochostos ('in the sand') current until 13th century; thereafter known only by the Frankish name Famagusta, Famagosta, etc.

Description

Harbour town and important fortress on the east coast of Cyprus, successor to the ancient settlement

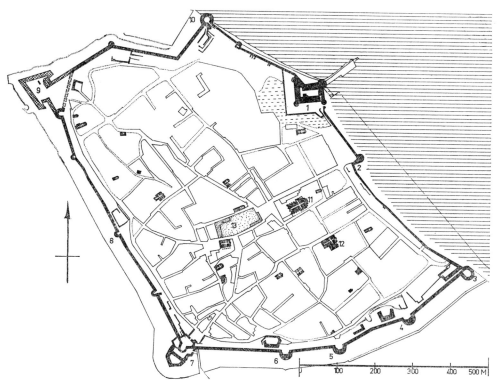

Plan 31: FAMAGUSTA. *Reconstruction of the town as it was at about the middle of the 16th century, scale 1:10,000. Late 15th- and early 16th-century fortifications in black, mid-16th-century buildings cross-hatched. 1, Citadel (Iç kale, also sea-fort). 2, Sea-gate. 3, Arsenal Bastion. 4, Campo Santo Bastion. 5, Andruzzi Bastion. 6, Santa Napa Bastion. 7, Inland Gate and ravelin. 8, Moratto Bastion. 9, Martinengo Bastion. 10, Diamond Bastion. 11, Latin Cathedral of St Nicholas (Aya Sofya Camii). 12, Greek Cathedral of St George. 13, Site and remains of former royal palace. (Based on Report of the Dept. of Antiquities, Cyprus.)*

of Salamis-Constantia, a few miles further along the coast to the north.

Although the interior of the town became nearly depopulated because of its unhealthy climate, the fortifications, which largely date from the Venetian period, are in good condition, as are the numerous churches. Famagusta stands on almost level ground beside a bay which is well protected by projecting reefs and could, in the Middle Ages, be sealed off by a chain suspended between the castle and a block-tower.

The lay-out of the town does not conform to any recognizable plan. It was enclosed by irregular curtains reinforced with bastions, the only heavily fortified section of this defensive perimeter being the two corners, i. e., the south-west inland gate and barbican dating from 1544, and the so-called Martinengo Bastion (c. 1550–60) in the north-west, constructed in the 'Old Italian' style. In the centre of the seaward face stands the citadel, known during the Turkish period as Iç kale or 'inner fortress'. The

nucleus of the citadel dates from the 14th century, whereas the outer wall was built in 1492, after Cyprus had been acquired by Venice.

History

1191. The small harbour town, which had waned in importance since the decline of Salamis-Constantia, is occupied by Richard Cœur de Lion and Guy de Lusignan.

1232. Philippe de Novare captures the tower guarding the harbour in the course of fighting between supporters of Emperor Frederick II and Cypriot royalists.

1291. After the fall of Acre, King Henry II (1285–1324) offers to resettle the Frankish fugitives in Famagusta and begins to strengthen the town's fortifications.

1306–10. Work on the defences is pursued with particular zeal during the brief reign of the usurper,

Amalric of Tyre, who completes the castle, makes additions to the royal palace and town, improves the sea-wall between the sea-gate and Arsenal Bastion in the south-east, and lays ditches with the aid of peasants conscripted from all over the island.

1336. Ludolf of Suchem refers to Famagusta as one of the wealthiest towns in the Levant. It now boasts the large cathedral of St Nicholas, built between 1308 and 1315.

1373. The Genoese capture Famagusta after a brief siege. It remains in their possession until 1463, despite numerous attempts by the kings of Cyprus to recapture it.

1464. After some three years of siege, Famagusta is restored to the royal house by a treaty with James II, 'The Bastard', but before long the Venetians have become firmly established there.

1488. Francisco Priuli raises the Venetian flag at Famagusta, and in the following year the Republic forces the last queen of Cyprus, Caterina Cornaro, to abdicate and renounce her title to the island.

1492–6. The Venetians improve the town defences, reconstructing the citadel's outer wall and the sea-gate. The Moratto Bastion is built under the direction of Niccolo Foscarini and Niccolo Priuli.

1544–c. 1565. Further improvements to the defences, including the reinforcement of the inland gate and the building of Martinengo Bastion.

1570–1. A Turkish army led by Lala Mustapha Pasha lands in Cyprus and lays siege to Famagusta. Under the command of Marco Antonio Bragadino, the town holds out heroically for almost a year but is forced to surrender on 29 July 1571, after the south face has been damaged by Turkish mines and supplies of food and ammunition are exhausted.

The few surviving Christian inhabitants are re-settled in the small village of Varosha, south of Famagusta, but are banned from entering the town walls after nightfall for several decades to come.

1572. Famagusta's defences are repaired after its capture. The buildings in the town gradually deteriorate in the ensuing decades, the harbour becomes silted up, and Famagusta loses its erstwhile importance as the islands's chief harbour.

Bibliography:
Enlart, *Art Gothique I*, 250–394, II 606–622;
G. Jeffery, *Historic Monuments of Cyprus*, Nicosia 1918;
A. H. S. Megaw, T. Mogabgab and others in the 1936–9 issues of the *Report of the Department of Antiquities, Cyprus*.

KOLOSSI   Plates 143–144

Gr. Kolossi; Frk. Le Colos, Colosso, etc.

Description

Castle and village in southern Cyprus, situated about six miles west of Limassol on the road to Paphos. All that remains of the small castle's defences is its massive donjon. South of this tower are some ruined outbuildings, and immediately to the east a vaulted structure with strong buttresses, the former sugar refinery, and the remains of a mill complete with mill-stream. There are cisterns in the basement of the three-storeyed donjon, magazines on the ground floor, an ante-room and kitchen on the first floor, and two vaulted living-rooms at the top.

History

1210. We have no precise information about the first castle to be built here, but the site may previously have been occupied by a small Byzantine stronghold. A castle was certainly in existence when the place was bestowed on the Hospitallers by King Hugh I.

1291–1301. The Hospitallers withdraw to Limassol after the fall of Acre and soon decide to develop Kolossi as another seat of their Order. Although this decision is never implemented because of the move to Rhodes, Kolossi remains the seat of the Grand

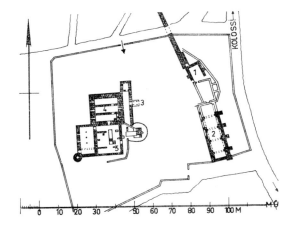

Plan 32: KOLOSSI. *Ground-plan of the Hospitaller estate, scale 1:2000. 1, Mill and mill-stream. 2, Former sugar refinery. 3 and 5, Outbuildings. 4, Donjon (Based on A. H. S. Megaw.)*

Commander of Cyprus and the centre of a rich Hospitaller estate incorporating many villages and vineyards.

Late 14th-early 15th centuries. Kolossi suffers as a result of numerous raids on the fertile region round Limassol (by the Genoese in 1373 and 1402, and by Mamelukes from Egypt in 1425).

2nd half of 15th century. The existing donjon is built under the direction of Grand Commander Louis de Magnac (c. 1450–68). Apart from the arms of its builder, it bears those of Jerusalem, Cyprus, Lusignan, Armenia and the Grand Masters of the Order of St John, J. de Lastic and J. de Milly.

1488. After Cyprus is ceded to Venice, Giorgio Cornaro, brother of the last queen, Caterina, is granted the title of Grand Commander and a share of the Order's estate. The title remains in the family until it becomes extinct in 1799.

1567–8. Severe earthquake damage is sustained in the vicinity of Limassol, presumably by the castle and the other property of the Order as well.

1570. Cyprus and the Hospitaller estates pass into Turkish possession. The refinery building is repaired by Murat Pasha in 1591.

Bibliography:
Enlart, *Art Gothique II*, 683–695;
J. Richard, *Chypre sous les Lusignan*, Paris 1962, 67 et seq.

BUFFAVENTO
Plate 145

Frk.-Lat. Bufevent, Buffavent, etc.; also Leonte, Château du Lion, Château de la Reine.

Description

Castle on the northern coast of Cyprus, about six miles south-east of Kyrenia, situated among the steep crags of the northern range at an altitude of over 3000 feet. It is in visual communication with Kyrenia, Nicosia and the castle of Kantara, and because of its favourable position it served for many years as a place where bonfires were lit to signal the approach of unidentified ships. It comprised a lower fortress, built on the southern slope and containing magazines and accommodation for the garrison, and an upper fortress about eighty feet above. Its asymmetrical lay-out was wholly determined by the mountainous terrain.

History

The castle's early history remains obscure, the local tradition about its origin being a hotch-potch of incompatible historical facts.

1232. Buffavento is first referred to as a place of refuge used by Eschive de Montbéliard during the fighting between members of Emperor Frederick II's faction and supporters of her father-in-law, the Regent Jean I d'Ibelin. It remained in the hands of the Cypriot party and was not subjected to attack.

The castle played an equally unwarlike role in the ensuing decades. It was used almost exclusively as a place of detention for important prisoners, who often ended their days there.

1st half of 16th century. Like a number of other obsolete mountain fortresses, Buffavento was dismantled by the Venetian authorities to save maintenance costs.

Bibliography:
Enlart, *Art Gothique II*, 596–605;
Rey, *Arch. Militaire*, 249 and Pl. 24.

BODRUM
Plates 146–153

Gr. Halikarnassos, in Middle Ages Petrunion; Frk.-Lat. Castrum Sancti Petri, S. Pietro, etc., after the vulgar Gr. Petrunion; Turk. Bodrum.

Description

Castle and small sea-port on the south-west coast of Asia Minor, opposite the Greek island of Cos. The extensive castle precincts occupy a peninsula which separates the inner harbour from the broad Bay of Bodrum. Inhabited since time immemorial and known in the ancient world as Zephyrion, this peninsula was probably used as a rear base by the Byzantines in the early Middle Ages.

Work on the castle continued almost without a break during its 120 years of Frankish occupation. The defences originally consisted of two strong towers and a single certain wall, but an outer wall reinforced with towers was added at about the middle of the 15th century. After 1480 the landward flank was adapted for the mounting of cannons and strengthened with massive bastions.

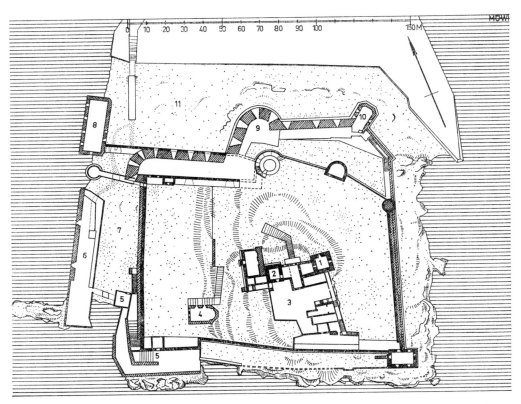

Plan 33: BODRUM – ST PETER (HALIKARNASSOS). *Ground-plan of the Hospitaller castle, scale 1:20,000 15th-century buildings in black, improvements (1501–22) hatched. 1, Tower of France. 2, Tower of Italy. 3, Inner bailey of original castle. 4, Chapel. 5, Inner gatehouse. 6, Large ravelin. 7, Forecourt. 8, Harbour Battery. 9, Carretto Bastion. 10, Gatineau Bastion. 11, Fosse. (Based on A. Maiuri, with author's additions.)*

History

1415. The Ottoman sultan Mehmet I grants the knights of Rhodes a site in Caria to compensate them for their expulsion from St Peter's Castle at Smyrna (modern Izmir). A new castle is built under the direction of the knight Schlegelholt, largely with materials taken from ancient buildings.

The Tower of France is the first to be constructed, followed *c.* 1431 by the Tower of Italy and, from about 1440 onwards, the strong north wall which traverses the peninsula and (in chronological order) the east, south and west flanks of the perimeter wall.

1480. After unsuccessfully attacking Rhodes, the Turks try to capture St Peter's but are repulsed.

1501–22. Further additions are made, including the harbour battery, north ditch and bastions, built partly with debris from the famous Mausoleum, one of the seven wonders of the ancient world. The chapel is erected in 1519-20.

1522. After losing Rhodes, the knights are forced to relinquish their other bases and withdraw, first to Italy and then to Malta. The castle is occupied by the Turks and used for centuries as a prison and small garrison base. It suffers severe damage when bombarded by a French fleet in 1915.

Bibliography:
G. Karo, 'Die Burg von Halikarnassos', in: *Archäolog. Anzeiger, 34,* 1919, 59–76;
A. Maiuri, 'I castelli dei Cavalieri di Rodi a Cos e a Budrum', in: *Annuario Scuola Atene 4/5,* 1921/22, 290 et seq.

RHODES

Plates 154–159

Gr. Rhodos; Frk.-Lat. Rhodi, Rhodes, Rode, castrum et burgus Rodi, and other variants.

Description

Town and fortress situated at the northern end of the principal island in the Dodecanese of the same name, and headquarters of the Order of St John for more than two centuries after its expulsion from the Holy Land.

The core of the original urban area beside the ancient main harbour was rebuilt by the Hospitallers during the first half of the 14th century and heavily fortified thereafter. Thanks to its good state of preservation and the extensive restoration work which has been undertaken in the past fifty years, it affords a good idea of the architecture of Frankish towns in the Levant and can, as the sole surviving example of these, serve at least as a partial guide to the erstwhile appearance of coastal towns in Syria and

Palestine. Originally designed on the medieval pattern (a system of main and outer walls with projecting towers), the defences had to be strengthened to facilitate the mounting of ordnance and adapted to withstand new methods of siegecraft after the first Turkish attack in 1480. The surviving fortifications are typical of the transition to early Italian forms of the modern bastion system.

History

Once a prosperous commercial centre, Rhodes was captured by the Arabs in 654. It was soon recaptured by the Byzantines, however, and remained in their possession, a small and sparsely inhabited sea-port, until seized by the Hospitallers. The knights, who had fled to Cyprus after the fall of Acre, embarked on the conquest of the island in 1306, after making a brief landing on the coast of Asia Minor (at Makri/Fethiye).

1310. Siege and capture of the town by Grand Master Fulco de Villaret, who immediately starts to improve its defences. Work on the fortifications pro-

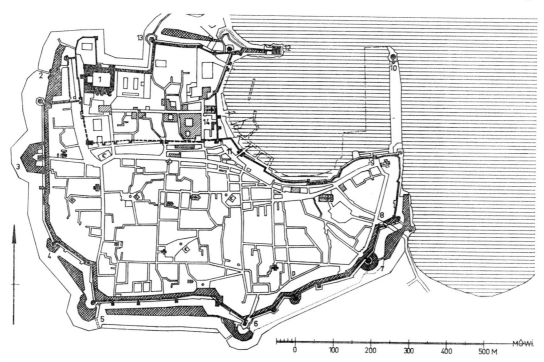

Plan 34: RHODES. *Reconstruction of town as in c. 1520, scale 1:10,000. Fortifications of 1314-1480 in black, additions of 1481-1522 cross-hatched. 1, Grand Master's Palace. 2, D'Amboise Gate. 3, St George's Bastion. 4, Spanish Bastion. 5, Santa Maria Bastion. 6, Koskinu Gate. 7, Italian Bastion. 8, Side-gate. 9, Santa Catharina Gate. 10, Mill-tower. 11, Porta Marina (Harbour gate). 12, Foundations of Naillac Tower. 13, St Peter's Bastion. 14, Hospital and Church of Ste Marie du Château. (Based on A. Gabriel.)*

ceeds almost without interruption under successive Grand Masters, both in Rhodes and later in the Hospitaller castle at Bodrum.

1314. Thus far, rebuilding has been limited to the 'castrum' or inner town, containing the Grand Master's Palace and the living-quarters of the various national contingents of the Order.

Mid-14th century. The urban area is enlarged by the addition of the so-called Burgus, or outer residential quarter, probably under the supervision of Grand Master Dieudonné de Gozon.

Early 15th century. Numerous parts of the defences, notably a large harbour block-tower, are rebuilt or newly constructed during the incumbency of Grand Master Philibert de Naillac. This work continues under his successor, Antonio Fluviano, and the two southern gates are reinforced in response to a threatened Egyptian invasion of Rhodes.

1437. Since the danger of an Egyptian attack persists under the next Grand Master, Jean de Lastic, the west and south flanks of the town's defences are strengthened.

1444. An Egyptian fleet lands and the town is besieged for over six weeks. Like a previous assault in 1440, this invasion proves fruitless, and the Egyptians are forced to withdraw.

1455-6. Battles are fought between the knights and the Turks, who invade the island but do not attack the town.

c. 1460. The town's defences are further reinforced by the addition of a continuous outer wall. Grand Master Raymond Zacosta erects the outlying fort of San Nicola on the spit of land separating the so-called Mandraki harbour from the main harbour.

In view of continuing Turkish threats and raids, the defences are substantially strengthened by Zacosta's successors, Giovanni Orsini and, more especially, Pierre d'Aubusson.

1479. After protracted negotiations between the knights and the Turks have broken down, a new Turkish fleet attacks Rhodes in the autumn but is driven off.

1480. The Turks attack again in greater strength, but the knights manage to withstand a severe 89-day

siege and bombardment thanks to a tactical blunder on the part of the Turkish admiral.

Immediately after the Turkish fleet has withdrawn, repairs and improvements are made to the fortifications under the energetic supervision of Grand Master Pierre d'Aubusson.

1481. The town and fortifications are badly damaged by an earthquake.

1512 onwards. Further improvements to the defences on the south and west flanks, including the construction of the Italian Bastion (1515) and St George's Bastion (1521 onwards). All the gates are rebuilt and the thickness of the walls is increased from 17 feet to approx. 40 feet. A second fosse and terreplein are laid between the two existing ditches.

1522. The town is again attacked by a strong Turkish army and fleet. The siege lasts from the end of July until 21 December, when, with all hope of relief gone and stocks of ammunition exhausted, the knights are forced to surrender in return for a guarantee of safe-conduct. They withdraw to Viterbo and Civitavecchia, and are later granted the island of Malta by Emperor Charles V.

Once in Turkish hands, Rhodes loses its importance as a fortress because the Hospitallers' departure leaves the whole of the Aegean under Turkish sovereignty. Their departure also puts an end to the sporadic proposals for further 'Crusades' against the Turks.

Bibliography:

A. Gabriel, La Cité de Rhodes, Vol. I: Architecture militaire, Paris 1921; Vol. II: Architecture civile et réligieuse, Paris 1923 (a compilation of all earlier research and sources);

A. Maiuri – G. Jacopi, 'Monumenti di Arte Cavalleresca', in: Clara Rhodos I, 1928;

P. Lojacono, 'Il Palazzo del Gran Maestro in Rodi', in: Clara Rhodos I, 1928;

R. Matton, Rhodes (Villes et paysages de Grèce), Athens 1959 (brief summary with limited bibliography).

NOTES ON THE PLATES

Numbers opposite the names of castles refer to pages in the foregoing section.

BELVAL

1. Tomb (*c.* late 12th century) from the ruined monastery of Belval (Vosges), now in the museum at Nancy; believed to represent Count Hugo de Vaudémont being greeted on his return from the Crusades by his wife, Hedwig von Dagsburg.

ISTANBUL

2. Towers forming part of the inland defences of Istanbul. The city walls of Constantinople were the first major fortifications to be encountered by the knights of the First Crusade after their march through the Balkans. The defensive perimeter, which is almost four miles long, consists of four successive barriers: a sixty-foot fosse with strong retaining walls, a low crenellated breastwork, an outer wall reinforced with semicircular and rectangular towers, and, finally, the main wall. The latter, which is constructed of rubble strengthened with a brickwork binding and faced with ashlar masonry, is reinforced throughout its length with ninety-six towers and possesses eight main and four subsidiary gates.
This plate shows Towers 17 and 18, which are situated between Golden Gate and Belgrat Kap in the southern part of the defensive perimeter.

IZNIK

3. South face of the town wall of Iznik (Nikaia, Nicaea). Nicaea was the first Seljuk-occupied stronghold encountered by the Franks after their army had assembled at Constantinople and crossed into Asia Minor. Supported by Byzantine troops and supervised by Byzantine military engineers, they besieged the heavily fortified town, directing the brunt of their attacks against the sector adjoining the south gate (now called the Yenişehir kapı, as illustrated). The so-called Gonatas Tower visible in the right-hand half of the picture was demolished by sapping, but the Byzantines, after negotiating with the Turks, occupied Nicaea the night before they and the Franks were due to launch a general assault – a step which scarcely enhanced the cordiality of Graeco-Frankish relations.
The walls visible in the foreground, together with the small semicircular tower and adjacent postern,

date from the period of Lascarid sovereignty, which began when the Franks captured Constantinople in 1204 and forced Emperor Theodore I Lascaris (1204–22) to withdraw to Nicaea. Theodore repaired the town walls and strengthened the whole perimeter by constructing an outer wall.

ANTAKYA

4. One of the main towers in the fortifications at Antioch, built on the elongated side of the Mons Silpius by Emperor Justinian (527–565). The city, which had suffered from earthquakes in 526 and 528 and sustained severe damage during the Persian conquest of 540, was completely re-fortified by Justinian, though on a greatly reduced scale. Its defences were only slightly altered in the ensuing centuries, but they formed one of the first major obstacles in the path of the first Crusader army. The Seljuk-held city was besieged from October 1097 until June 1098, when it was captured as a result of treachery on the part of a junior commander.
This photograph clearly illustrates the technique used by the builders of the wall, which is about 7½ miles long and was reputed to have been guarded by 360 towers. Its upper and lower sections were built of ashlar blocks filled with concrete-like masonry (known as *opus incertum),* and the extremely hard mortar used in its construction made it very durable. It was reinforced, approximately in the centre, by eight lacing-courses of brickwork which extended the full depth of the wall.
A roughly similar technique was employed in most of the towers forming part of the town defences, which were not demolished until the 19th century. Although in widespread use during the Byzantine period, this technique was not common in the Syrian area and betrays the influence of the capital.

JERUSALEM

5. View of the Old City from the tower of St Saviour's, which stands on the site of the erstwhile Hospital of St John. In the centre of the picture is the large quarter called Harâm eš-Šerîf, on the left the old Temple precincts and the Dome of the Rock, and on the right the Mosque of El-Aqṣâ. The Dome of the Rock – one of the most important shrines in the Islamic world – was transformed into a church (the Templum Domini) after the capture of Jerusalem in 1099 but restored to Islam when Saladin regained the city in 1187. It remained in Muslim hands during the period 1229–1244, even after Jerusalem had been reacquired by Emperor Frederick II. The Mos-

que of El-Aqṣâ started life as a church but was converted into a mosque after the first Arab conquest of Jerusalem in 638. Under the Franks, it became first a royal palace and then, in 1118, the seat of the Order of the Temple. To the west (i. e. this side) of the mosque can be seen a section of the old Jewish wailing wall, in front of which (roughly at the right-hand edge of the picture) once stood the Hospital of the Teutonic Order.

In the background is the Mount of Olives with the Garden of Gethsemane and a small Russian monastery at its foot, and below, the valley of the Kedron (Wâdî Sitti Maryam).

6. The north face of the city walls of Jerusalem. It was on this front, where the lie of the land has always presented the best opportunities for attack, that the knights of the first Crusader army succeeded on 15 July 1099, after almost six weeks of siege, in propelling one of their large siege-towers close enough to the wall to storm the parapet. Saladin concentrated his attack on more or less the same sector in 1187, damaging the walls so badly by sapping them and bombarding them with mangonels that the garrison was forced to yield.

The existing walls date from the years 1531–41, when the city was re-fortified by the Ottoman sultan Süleyman I (1520–66). No alterations were made to the lay-out of the walls, but their superstructure was heightened and partially renovated so as to render the city defensible against surprise attack.

7. West face of the Mosque of El-Aqṣâ in Temple Square (Harâm eš-Šerif). Allegedly built on the site of one of Justinian's churches and last restored by the Fatimid caliph aẓ-Ẓâhir in 1033, following damage by several earthquakes, the mosque was used as a royal palace after the Frankish conquest and known as the Templum Salomonis. Having been granted parts of the palace when their Order was founded by Hugues de Payen in 1118, the Templars acquired the whole building when the king moved out. After conquering the city in 1187, Saladin reconverted the seat of the Templars into a mosque and added to it. The north vestibule (on the left of the picture) was added by Sultan Malik al-Mu'aẓẓam in 1217–18. Much of the side-aisles and (probably) the outer walls of the present building were erected in the Frankish period. Pilgrims' accounts mention the founding of a church, but it was evidently never completed.

The dome and its inner substructure date from the earliest structural phase (1033).

8. Exterior façade of the Sitti Maryam Gate, seen from the east. According to an extant inscription above the entrance, it was erected in Year 945 of the Hegira, i. e., in 1538, during the reign of Sultan Süleyman I. The present gate embodies the remains of its predecessor. It stands at the end of the large street which forms the continuation of the Via Dolorosa, immediately to the north of Harâm eš-Šerif, and has been the only gateway leading to the Kedron Valley since the Golden Gate was walled up. Apart from the Arab name in current use today, the gate has borne many other names in the course of its history, notably Stephen's Gate, Jehosaphat Gate and Gethsemane Gate.

TRIPOLI   Page 42

9. General view of the castle from the east, looking across the deep bed of the Nahr Qadîša. The lower portions of the walls perched on the steep rocky slope consist of good Frankish masonry, but the upper portions date from Arab or even Turkish times.

10. Main gate of the castle, seen from the north. The narrow fosse was originally spanned by a drawbridge which gave access to the cramped gate-yard. Erected at the beginning of the 14th century, probably on earlier foundations, the gate was restored in 1521 (according to an inscription above the entrance) by the Ottoman sultan Süleyman I. the Magnificent.

11. Frankish remains (a pillar forming part of a hall or chapel?) in the south face of the large interior courtyard, built into the outer wall of a vaulted building dating from the early 14th century. On the right, a small Islamic tomb.

SAHYUN   Page 44

12. Aerial view (1938) of the castle precincts taken from the west. On the left are the simple fortifications of the spacious lower fortress, which follow the lie of the land; clearly distinguishable in the centre are the massive towers of the upper fortress, and, on the summit of the ridge, the old Byzantine citadel. The rocky spur facing the castle in the north (foreground) was where Saladin mounted the catapults with which he bombarded Sahyun in 1188.

13. Interior view of the main (north-east) defensive front (for an exterior view v. colour plate 3). In the centre of the picture is the massive donjon, approximately 82 feet square, and on the right the first tower of the south face. The inner side of this tower abuts on one of the earlier Byzantine walls, whose small stonework clearly differentiates it from the walls of the Frankish period, which were built of heavy blocks of boss-and-margin masonry.

14. The south face, showing the round corner-bastion and two of the three large rectangular towers on

this flank. At the foot of the vertical rock-face, which was artificially cut away, runs the main track leading to the castle.

15. The deep fosse, hewn out of the solid rock, is overlooked by a massive wall dating from various Frankish structural periods. In the centre towers the equally massive donjon, entirely faced with smooth ashlar-work. The smooth stonework immediately above the vertically-hewn rock-face hails from a somewhat earlier structural phase than the upper parts of the walls, where there is a transition to boss-and-margin ashlar-work of different types. The two-storeyed donjon has two exterior defensive galleries as well, making a total of four tiers of loopholes.

16. The fosse, showing the drawbridge support in the middle. The pillar was formed by hewing away the surrounding rock and topped with masonry for added height.

17. The lower chamber of the donjon, with a heavy cross-vaulted ceiling and a central pillar roughly ten feet square. Partially unearthed remains of the Byzantine outer wall can be seen at its foot.

18. The Byzantine inner citadel. In the foreground are ruined medieval living-quarters of varying date. Behind them stands the innermost Byzantine perimeter wall with the inner citadel towering high above it, a donjon-type building of wholly asymmetrical design.

19. The inner courtyard of the upper fortress, seen from the south. The minaret in the foreground belongs to a late 13th-century mosque, and behind it is the Byzantine cross-wall and the donjon.

20. View of one the aisles in the large magazine adjoining the donjon in the south. Above the old Byzantine outer wall stands a large vaulted hall comprising five aisles, each of five bays. The freestone pillars, which measure approximately 6 feet by 7, support rough stone cross-vaults closely interspersed with heavy groined freestone arches for greater structural strength.

21. The inner chamber of the large cistern on the northern flank of the upper fortress. The lower part of the cistern was hewn out of the solid rock and the walls plastered with watertight mortar. The low wall above supports a heavy barrel-vaulted roof constructed of neatly fitted voussoirs. The corbels acted as supports for scantlings.

QAL'AT SUBEIBE   Page 45

22. General view of the castle from the south, facing the mountains. In the foreground are the towers of the short south face, badly damaged by earthquakes, and behind them in the interior the ruins of a small deserted village. In the background, separated from the spacious lower bailey by a cross-wall, rises the citadel, a massive edifice with corner-bastions, possibly embodying architectural relics of the Byzantine period.

AL-KERAK   Page 47

23. Castle and town of Kerak from the south-east, with the Wâdî as-Sitt in the foreground. On the left is the deep fosse and birket (open cistern); adjoining it on the right can be seen the lofty donjon, built on the summit of a steep revetted slope, together with the east face of the upper fortress, almost all of which dates from the Frankish period, although only the lower part of the corner-tower facing the north fosse still survives. In the right-hand third of the picture is the town wall, most of the upper portions of which originated in the post-1188 period.

24. South-west prospect from the Wâdî al-frangî. In the background (left), the western flank of the town fortifications. Apart from the walls of the birket (reservoir) and a small section of the wall adjoining it, all the fortifications visible in this picture -- notably the large polygonal donjon -- are post-Frankish additions.

25. Southern flank of the town walls, with the castle keep in the left background. The lower portions of the wall visible in the foreground hail largely from the Frankish period, whereas most of the superstructure was rebuilt at various stages during the second half of the 13th century.

26. Upper bailey of the castle, looking southwards at the large donjon. Preserved beneath the present level of the courtyard are the remains of Frankish living-quarters, some of which can be discerned in the foreground.

The polygonal ground-plan and terraced superstructure of the five-storeyed donjon render it one of the most interesting buildings of its type. The exterior walls are more than sixteen feet thick.

27. Lower bailey of the castle. On the left, perched above a wall of rock which has been partially hewn away by hand, is the west wall of the upper fortress. Apart from the two rectangular bastions, this dates from the Frankish period. The western flank of the outer wall of the lower fortress, with its skilfully designed west gate, was not built until after the Arab conquest.

Structural phases, mainly distinguishable by variations in the colour of the materials employed, can also be differentiated -- though with less clarity -- by variations in stone-mason's technique. Structural components of the Arab period ordinarily display greater care in the dressing of masonry.

BAĞRAS   Page 48

28. General view of the tall, compact castle, taken from the south. One can still see, on the left, the point at which the outer enceinte was joined by an aqueduct (no longer extant).
29. View of the large (north) hall and the retaining wall of the upper courtyard adjoining it on the left, taken from the lower inner courtyard. On the right, the entrance to the large magazine vaults, which also helped to terrace the confined areas of courtyard in the upper fortress.
30. View of the large south-west defensive gallery, which is accessible from the lower fortress. In the foreground are the remains of an earlier structure built of large, roughly-dressed blocks of stone.
31. Taken from the upper inner courtyard, this photograph shows the south hall and, beyond it, the broad plain surrounding Lake Amq. Hârim is just over twenty miles away as the crow flies. In the foreground are vaults which once formed the substructure of the upper courtyard.

AKKAR   Page 50

32. The castle, seen from the valley of the Nahr 'Akkâr in the north. At the northern extremity of the castle rock stands a retaining wall of good dressed stonework which evidently supported a building of some size. Remnants of the old perimeter wall extend southwards to a ruined tower which stands on a projecting spur of rock to the east. The donjon and the main flank of the castle, which faces the mountains, cannot be seen in this photograph.

TARTUS   Page 50

33. Interior façade of a rectangular bastion in the inner enceinte. Of the long vaulted passages which originally zig-zagged round the main defensive perimeter, all that survive are stretches of outer wall embodying supports for wooden ceilings.
    The whole exterior of the citadel's perimeter wall was carefully faced with smooth or boss-and-margin ashlar blocks.
34. West face of the cathedral (a museum since 1960).
35. Interior of the cathedral. Like the cross-vaulted aisles, the pointed barrel-vaulting of the nave is divided into five sections by heavy groined arches supported by pillars with half-columns. On each side of the apse, with its semi-dome-shaped vaulting, are small subsidiary chambers.
    The pillar visible in the centre of the picture rests on an archway which may have been the pilgrims' entrance to an earlier shrine.

SAFITA   Page 51

36. General view from the east, with the ruins of the large gate in the foreground. When this picture was taken (1936) the substructure of the outer curtain wall was still visible in the unbuilt-up areas west and north of the donjon, but this has largely been built over or demolished in the intervening years.
37. Westward-facing view of the large hall-cum-gateway to the east of the donjon, a two-storeyed structure of which only the west wall and remains of vaulting have survived.
38. The donjon, showing main access. The walls, which are constructed of excellent ashlar-work, show distinct traces of the repairs carried out after the great earthquake of 1202, during which the upper storey and part of the left-hand corner of the building collapsed.
39. The large hall on the first floor of the donjon. Clear evidence of early 13th-century design can be discerned in the pillars, which are elaborately segmented by projecting pilasters, and in the heavy cross-vaulting.

QAL'AT YAHMUR   Page 52

40. General view from the south. On the left, one of the corner-towers which were added later, and behind it the massive two-storeyed donjon.
41. Entrance to the donjon (probably restored during the Arab period). The ground and first floors of the tower contain large vaulted chambers. The upper superstructure has almost entirely collapsed, but it is probable that the tower was surmounted by a low two-tiered defensive gallery which considerably augmented its height.

ARIMA   Page 53

42. General view from the east, clearly showing how the precincts were divided into separate terraces. At the summit of the long ridge stands the upper fortress, with its main defensive front pointing south.
43. Interior face of the main tower beside the gate leading to the citadel, seen from the inner bailey. Adjoining it on the right are the remains of a sizable hall.

BA'ALBEK   Page 54

44. General view from the south. The precinct walls of the Temple of Jupiter, which tower above the broad plain, did not require strengthening when the place was converted into a fortress. The existing walls

were simply pierced with loopholes and topped with battlements. The exposed southwest flank, incorporating the level site of the Temple of Bacchus, had to be substantially reinforced with a curtain wall to which several towers were added at a later stage.

45. Medieval additions to the large hexagonal forecourt of the Temple of Jupiter. The windows above the lower gallery, which used to be richly embellished with pillars and timberwork, were converted into loopholes.

46. Southern façade of the Temple of Bacchus from the east. Beyond the gateway (improved at the end of the 13th century) is the south-west corner-tower (1213), and behind the temple's corner-colums can be seen the junction of the strong west curtain-wall which, like the corner-tower, originated in the time of Bahrâm-Shâh.

The south face of the temple was fortified during the first phase of reconstruction by a wall which ran partly between the columns and partly in front of the stylobate. This wall was demolished in the course of excavation. The temple's south face was also protected by a wide fosse.

SHEIZAR

Page 55

47. Castle and village from the north (1937). At the northern tip of the ridge, in front of a revetted construction of manifestly earlier date, stands the great gatehouse of Sultan Qala'ûn. The isolated fragments of the long east wall which are discernible in this picture have since collapsed.

48. The donjon, viewed from the south side of the fosse. Beneath the tower on the left are remains of earlier fortifications which were destroyed in 1157. Clearly visible in the centre of the tower's façade is the line where the older portion (right) meets the more recent. Attempts were made to safeguard the tower against further earthquakes and enhance its stability by reinforcing its walls with columns taken from the ancient settlement.

49. Gatehouse, bearing an inscription attributing it to Sultan Qala'ûn.

QAL'AT EL-MUDIQ

Page 56

50. General view from the west (1933). On the slope on the right is the broad approach ramp, guarded by towers, and beside it are remains of the medieval revetment. Relics of earlier periods of habitation can be seen all over slopes, which have been heavily eroded in places.

51. Looking across the site of the ancient settlement at the southern and most heavily fortified flank of the town. The recent widening of the approach ramp has damaged parts of the old revetment and cut into the stratified debris of earlier civilizations. The towers on this flank, which had sustained earthquake damage, were evidently safeguarded against collapse in the Middle Ages by the addition of buttresses and corner-pillars.

MARQAB

Page 56

52. General view from the south (1938). The outer and inner perimeter walls of the outer fortress can be clearly seen on the projecting spur in the west. On the flat saddle at the foot of the citadel (not visible in this photograph) is a large rectangular *birket* or reservoir. The road running up the slope on the left is modern. The old approach road lies slightly higher and leads to the gate-tower in the centre of the south-west face.

Beside the bay in the background stand the houses of the small port of Bâniyâs, once the seat of a Latin archbishop and known during the Frankish period as Valenia.

53. Old approach road and view of the south-west face of the inner fortress.

54. Approach to outer gate-tower. Strengthened in modern times, the approach road runs across a bridge (with massive walls, probably of more recent construction) into the gatehouse, which was partially altered in Arab times. Access to the entrance was guarded by machicolated extensions above it. On the right, the archway of the inner main gate.

55. View of the north inner courtyard from the roof of the castle chapel. In the background, more or less in the centre of the picture, stands the outer gate-tower, and in front of it are the remains of a hall with a carefully constructed vaulted roof (now entirely demolished). The large arch in the foreground may have been added when the main gate was altered by the Turks, probably to render it easier of access.

Grouped round the inner courtyard are barrack and store rooms, some of them badly dilapidated.

56. The spacious bailey of the inner fortress. On the left, a long row of vaulted chambers; in the centre of the picture, the side wall and side entrance of the castle chapel.

57. Side entrance of the chapel, almost identical with the main portal but in better condition. The erstwhile porch collapsed during one of the many earthquakes. Profiles and capitals bear a strong resemblance to French examples dating from the latter half of the 12th century.

58. West face of the chapel, showing the elaborate ornamentation of the main portal, whose sparse but somewhat ponderous detail is typical of design in the Frankish Levant at the turn of the 12th-13th centuries. The lower part of the chapel's outer walls are surfaced with small, neat basalt blocks, whereas the upper courses are of the usual rubble-work. As in other parts of the castle, the portals and window surrounds are carved in softer limestone.

59. The castle chapel, looking towards the apse. With its heavy cross-vaulting divided by a central groined arch, the single-naved building is reminiscent of the somewhat ponderous High Romanesque architecture of Southern France, which doubtless exerted a powerful influence on building in the Holy Land.
   The chapel was long used as the episcopal church of the Latin Bishop of Valenia, who lived in the castle for reasons of security.

60. The Burǧ aṣ-Ṣabî ('Boy's Tower', so called after an ancient legend), situated below Marqab beside the sea. An outwork forming part of the castle's defences, this three-storeyed tower was designed to protect the small harbour of Margat and block the coast road. According to unconfirmed reports, it was once linked with the castle.

61. Distant view. Taken from the coast road, this photograph illustrates the castle's commanding position.

QAL'AT ADJLUN   Page 58

62. Distant view of the castle from the south-east, looking across the deep bed of the Wâdî Kefrinja.

63. The south-east face, showing the gatehouse (right) and the massive south tower, which dates from the second structural phase. Its boss-and-margin masonry reposes directly on the rock itself.

64. The north-west face. In the foreground is the upper fortress with its inset west corner-tower and half-ruined north corner-tower – all built of small, neatly dressed ashlar blocks resting on older boss-and-margin stonework. Only the north corner-tower of the outer fortress has retained its original appearance.

65. Interior courtyard, showing the old main entrance to the inner fortress, which was substantially altered at the beginning of the 13th century. Also dating from this phase of reconstruction is the stonework visible on the right, a small flight of steps leading to the entrance of the large south tower and the west wall of what later became the gatehouse.

KRAK DES CHEVALIERS   Page 59

66. General view taken from the south-east in 1931, during the early stages of its excavation and restoration by the French. The houses of the small village have not yet been demolished, and the castle presents almost the same appearance as it did towards the end of the 19th century.

67. View from the north-east.

68. South outer face. In the foreground, fortifications constructed after the Arab conquest. On the left, the round-tower erected in 1271, during the reign of Sultan Baibars, and next to it the aqueduct; on the right, the large rectangular tower built by Sultan Qala'ûn. Both towers carry long inscriptions beneath the consoles of their machicolated galleries.

69. Large revetment in front of the south face of the upper fortress. Behind the revetted slope, which is faced with smooth ashlar blocks, are two tiers of vaulted galleries equipped with loopholes.

70. South-west corner-tower of the upper fortress, containing the so-called Logis du Maître.

71. View from the south forecourt, showing the block-tower which was probably built during the last Frankish structural phase. This enabled the defenders to guard the approaches to the upper fortress and enfilade the fosse and forecourt.

72. Taken from the gate of the block-tower, this view shows the fosse and the reverse face of the tower built by Sultan Qala'ûn, together with the adjacent magazines and stables. Both sides of the fosse were neatly faced with stone because it also served as a water reservoir.

73. The upper part of the covered approach, whose vaulted roof abuts on the substructure of the south-east corner-tower of the upper fortress. The vaulted ceiling runs almost the entire length of the passage, which twists and turns sharply and was guarded by additional barriers and enfilading positions.

74. Entrance to the lower bailey of the inner fortress, with a view of the Great Hall (mid-13th century).

75. Looking into the vestibule of the Great Hall, which was used as a chapter-house. The wealth of architectural detail is directly related to French prototypes.

76. Looking southwards across the lower bailey of the upper fortress. On the left, the façade of the Great Hall; opposite it, the upper gatehouse, and projecting above and beyond it the castle chapel with its open vestibule. The flat roofs of all the buildings were faced with stone slabs or rubble-work for collecting rain-water.

77. The spacious forecourt to the west of the castle. On the right, the long western flank of the upper fortress, bordered – like the south face – by a continuous revetment surmounted by vaulted defensive galleries. On the left, the interior face of the outer curtain wall, the upper courses of which have entirely disintegrated.

78. Main chamber of the south-west corner-tower, known as the Logis du Maître. It was converted into

living accommodation *c*. 1230–40, when the existing loopholes were blocked up and replaced by a large window on the east side.

79. Capital and frieze of rosettes in the Logis du Maître.

80. Lower bailey of the upper fortress. On the left, one corner of the Great Hall; on the right, the open vestibule of the castle chapel; in the background, the massive north tower.

81. Interior of the castle chapel, facing the apse. The single chamber has a heavy barrel-vaulted ceiling and is divided into three sections by thick groined arches. The walls are segmented by recessed blind arches and by a continuous cornice which emphasizes the springing line. After the Arab conquest the chapel was converted into a small mosque. The small semicircular niches in the south wall and the covered steps (miḥrâb) date from this period.

82. Vestibule of the Great Hall, displaying an architectural elaboration rarely found in castles of the Frankish Levant. The builders of such castles generally abstained from outward show and limited themselves to the neat and workmanlike construction of what was necessary for defensive purposes.

83. South portal of the Great Hall. Individual features of this building are in full accord with those present in examples of mid-13th-century architecture in France, e. g., at Rheims.

BEAUFORT   Page 62

84. General view from the west (1936). In the foreground are relics of a medieval settlement, and beyond them, hewn deep into the solid rock, lies the broad fosse, which opens out into a *birket* or reservoir at its northern extremity. On the right, rising abruptly out of the fosse, are the smoothly revetted bases of the two corner-towers belonging to the southern outworks built at the turn of the 12th-13th centuries. Above and to the left is the boss-and-margin stonework facing of the outer wall and the similarly constructed donjon (first half of 12th century). The polygonal hall whose remains can be seen at the northern tip of the site (left) dates from the first Arab occupation.

JEBAIL   Page 64

85. General view of the town and castle of Jebail, with the modern harbour in the foreground and the medieval harbour fort on the right. On the left, the Frankish church of St John (1115–*c*. 1200), once the town's principal church.

86. Inner face of the harbour fort and remains of the old mole. Parts of the fort were covered up when the mole was substantially widened in recent times. It originally consisted of two strong towers linked by a massive wall. Parts of the superstructure of the inner tower can still be seen on the left, but the only relics of the stronger outer tower are some isolated fragments of the foundations, which are visible on the shelf of rock in front of the fort.

87. West exterior face of the castle and south fosse. The fosse, which used to run the entire perimeter of the castle, was filled in and its retaining wall demolished when the ancient Phoenician town wall was being excavated. Beside the north-west corner-tower (left) is one of the numerous sally-ports. The adjoining curtain-wall is built of neatly-worked boss-and-margin masonry, and its lower courses were reinforced by the insertion of ancient columns, laid transversely. The two corner-towers visible on the right have been partially restored in modern times. The upper part of the donjon, which used to consist entirely of massive blocks of stone, was repaired during the Turkish occupation with the smaller stonework typical of that period. The open hall to the left of the donjon also dates from that time.

HARIM   Page 65

88. Bird's-eye view of castle and town from the north-east (1935). Almost all the ruined buildings in the interior of the spacious lower fortress have since disappeared, as have large sections of the so-called citadel. The old approach road running up the hillside (left) is still in use today.

89. General view, showing the broad plain round Lake Amq and the Amanus Mountains in the background. The plain abounds in hills which – like Hârim – have been gradually augmented by centuries of human habitation (Arab. *tell*, Turk. *hüyük*, proving that this area was the home of a highly developed early civilization.
The fortifications, which originally encircled the summit of the hill with little to break their outline save the defensive core in the north-east, must have resembled the well-preserved citadel at Aleppo.

ALEPPO   Page 67

90. Aerial photograph of the citadel from the east (1936), with the extensive vaulted bazaar *(sûq)* in the background and – at the upper edge of the picture – the Great Mosque, situated in the centre of the medieval city. The rigidly rectangular ground-plan of the ancient city is clearly discernible in the parallel course of the main thoroughfares and bazaar streets.

91. Main gate of the citadel from the south-west. The earliest portions of the gatehouse are the rectangular bastions on either side of the gateway. These originally stopped short at the upper edge of the machicolated gallery and were not incorporated into a single tower until the large hall on the upper floor was built.

The skilfully designed gatehouse is approached by a bridge resting on five massive columns, and access to it is guarded by an outer gate built in the early 16th century. The escarpment round the citadel used to be faced with large blocks of masonry. This revetment is still in good condition in the vicinity of the gate.

BOSRA   Page 67

92. Town and citadel in original condition (1934). Upper sections of the *scaenae frons* and tiers of spectators' seats are clearly visible above the medieval additions, as is the forecourt between the exterior façade of the ancient theatre and the wall erected in front of it. The fosse which once surrounded the entire site has largely been filled in.

93. View of the raised forecourt with the outer wall of the ancient theatre on the right and the towers of the outer defences (1211–51) on the left.

94. Main entrance to the citadel. The approach road runs across a narrow bridge into an outer forecourt guarded by two towers, and from there, *en chicane*, through the tower visible at the right-hand edge of the picture and into the interior of the fortress.

MASYAF   Page 68

95. General view of the castle from the east, showing the terracing of the three separate defensive perimeters: an outer ring enclosing the lower level, and above this two roughly concentric inner rings separated by a narrow forecourt. On the extreme left, the outworks which guarded the approaches, and above them the tall, stoutly constructed gate-tower. Almost every conceivable form of tower is represented in the castle, together with walls dating from different phases of construction and built in a wide variety of materials, from rough rubble-work to the finest ashlar blocks.

SAIDA – SIDON   Page 69

96. Town and harbour of Saidâ from the air (1938). On the right, the sole surviving large semicircular tower of the old citadel, which covered the southern flank of the town. The broad fosse in front of it has been excavated in recent years.

97. View of the small inner harbour, showing the harbour fort with its new bridge and freely restored gate façade. On the left, the main defensive tower, which probably dates from the Arab period (late 15th- or early 16th-centruy). On the right, above the gate, a small mosque built during the Turkish occupation.

CHASTEL PELERIN   Page 71

98. General view from the north-east. In the foreground, the northernmost tower of the town defences and remains of the simple wall. In the background, the only surviving tower in the strong cross-wall, built of fine quality stonework. Adjoining the tower on the right is the north bastion, which juts far into the sea (whose level may have sunk in the interim). These two-storeyed towers also functioned as gate-towers, but there was no communication between the gate-level and the defensive galleries above, which could only be reached from the inner fortress via the transverse walls which sealed off the ends of the forecourt.

ACRE   Page 72

99. Town and harbour from the south. On the extreme left, remains of the medieval mole and the sea-wall, parts of which also date from the Middle Ages. In the 19th century, the long curtain-wall beneath the two tall towers extended to meet the massive tower which rises above the wooden landing-stage, the Burǧ es-Sulṭân, dating from the Frankish period.

100. The so-called 'Crypt of the Knights of St John', a two-aisled vault beneath the Turkish barracks, which later became a prison. Situated in the Hospitaller quarter, this building was excavated in recent times. The heavily groined cross-vaults are supported by three massive pillars. The windows and doors in the side-walls indicate that the place was a ground-floor chamber rather than a crypt, but its original function has yet to be ascertained.

CAESAREA   Page 74

101. Outer entrance of the main gate on the west side of the town, one of the improvements made by King Louis IX (Saint-Louis). Originally a simple structure, the gate was given an angled entrance by the new outer chamber and additionally protected by a strong tower on the landward side.

102. South-east corner and adjoining southern flank of the town fortifications. The fosse, about 40 feet wide, was bordered on the landward side by a vertical wall of small stonework which followed the salients and re-entrants of the curtains and bastions. The lower part of the wall was reinforced by a strong talus with a slope of roughly 60 degrees.

103. The citadel on the southern mole, partially covered with modern houses, showing the ruins of the large donjon (ground-area approximately 62 feet square). Most of the outer walls have collapsed into the shallow harbour (left).

MONTFORT   Page 74

104. General view from the south-west. On the extreme right, the half-ruined fosse, together with the remains of the donjon and the semicircular talus at its foot. Unlike those of other castles, Montfort's was a free-standing donjon which lay in front of the wall and was only connected to the inner fortress by a drawbridge. Behind the jutting section of wall is the 'palace' and a lower courtyard dominated in the north by a tower.

105. Beyond the chapel can be seen the ruined donjon, its rear wall and the entrance on its south side (visible in Photograph 104). Differences in stonework reveal that the castle was added to at various stages. No details of its early history are known.

TOPRAKKALE   Page 75

106. General view from the west, showing the perimeter wall which encircles the hill about half-way up, and, towering high above it, the main defensive face of the upper fortress. Ruined walls of the ancient settlement can be seen on the slope on the right, beneath the outer perimeter wall. These walls helped supply material for the medieval castle.

107. Main defensive face of the upper fortress, with steep revetted flanks and a row of stout semicircular towers. Remains of the machicolated gallery which once ran along the entire front can be clearly seen on the right. The walls are built of rough basalt blocks and repose directly on the rock in places. The revetment dates from a later building period and contains a vaulted defensive gallery.

108. Ruins of a tower on the north flank of the upper fortress, once used as living-quarters.

SIS (KOZAN)   Page 77

109. The castle from the south. At the summit of the precipitate ridge stands a massive round-tower flanked by zigzag curtain-walls.

YILAN KALESI   Page 77

110. General view from the south, showing the gate-flank of the upper fortress above the deep valley of the Ceyhan.

CORYCUS   Page 79

111. General view of the fortifications from the landward side, showing the north face of the mainland castle with its twin walls, the small harbour, and the island fort.

112. View of the harbour, the ruined mole and the island fort, which was originally built in the Byzantine period but acquired its present appearance largely under Armenian sovereignty.

113. The mainland castle from the east. On the right, the most elaborate group of towers in the inner fortress and the Great Hall, its exterior reinforced by a large semicircular bastion.

114. The main, eastward-facing defensive front, showing the fosse, which was hewn out of the solid rock and could be partially flooded with sea-water.

SILIFKE   Page 80

115. Semicircular towers on the southern flank. On the left, the fosse, parts of which were hewn out of the solid rock, and remnants of the outer wall.

116. General view of the castle and town, seen across the broad expanse of the Gök-Su. The superstructure of the bridge is modern, but the foundations are Roman. The slopes in front of the castle were once occupied by an ancient settlement of which isolated fragments and rocky terraces are all that remain.

ANAMUR   Page 81

117. General view from the west. On the rocky headland stands the elaborate but badly dilapidated inner fortress, flanked on the left by the wall of the inner courtyard, which lies at a lower level.

BODONITSA   Page 82

118. Panoramic view of the broad Kallidromon highlands which lie between the Kephissos in Bœotia and the river Sperkhios, which flows into the Bay of Lamia. The small castle visible in the background is situated on the southern slopes.

CASTEL TORNESE   Page 82

119. The castle from the east.

120. The upper fortress from the east. In the centre, the gatehouse, adjoined by the upper perimeter wall

of the lower fortress. During a later phase of construction, the base of the upper fortress was reinforced against artillery bombardment by the addition of a sloping escarpment.

NAVARINO   Page 83

121. The south wall of the lower fortress, most of which dates from the Venetian occupation, seen through the outer gate. Together with the 'Batteria Morosina' beyond it, this wall straddles the remains of older buildings and terminates in the 'Posto Precipio', a round battery tower containing artillery case-mates.

122. Looking southwards from the upper fortress across the outer perimeter of the lower fortress, the outer gate (Porta da fortezza), and the small Venetian bastion of Santa Barbara. In the centre, the rocky island of Sphakteria (with relics of ancient forti-fications), separated from the mainland by a narrow channel. In the background on the extreme left, the fortress of New Navarino (now called Pylos), erected by the Turks in 1573 as a replacement for the old castle.

MISTRA   Page 84

123. Castle and town from the north. Below, left, the Monastery of Brontochion and the lower town wall, which dates from the Byzantine period. On the spur above, the Despots Palace. Guillaume de Villehardouin's castle occupies the summit of the steeply sloping ridge.

124. The upper town and steep castle hill, at the foot of which the Byzantine upper town wall ends. The projecting north-west bastion of the castle and massive gatehouse (on the extreme left) are clearly visible.

KARYTAINA   Page 85

125. Castle and village from the south. Perched on the crag on the far side of the Alpheios valley is the polygonal south bastion. On the slope (left), rem-nants of the lower fortress.

KANTARA   Page 85

126. General view from the south. The ground rises mo-derately steeply to the forecourt but falls away sharply elsewhere. The main defensive front and its two flanking semicircular towers are clearly visible beyond the semicircular bastions of the forecourt. In front of the forecourt, supported by strong buttresses, is an open cistern.

127. Main defensive front, showing main gate, semicir-cular west tower and outlying bastion.

128. Main defensive front from the interior, showing the large semicircular tower on the right and, on the left, the east tower, which was originally divided into three storeys for defensive purposes. A door leads out of the lower gallery into a narrow turret chamber with seven loopholes from which the en-tire forecourt could be raked with enfilading fire.

ST HILARION   Page 86

129. Looking down from the castle at the coast-line and small town of Kyrenia. The harbour and its large fort can be clearly distinguished.

130. The western flank of the castle, with the wall of the outer fortress running up the steep incline. Half-way up, Prince John's Tower. (A gruesome legend has it that the prince hurled the members of his Bulgarian bodyguard over the cliff one by one.) The upper fortress at the summit dates from the Frankish period, whereas the wall on the slope beneath is part of the earlier Byzantine fortifi-cations.

131. View of the lower fortress, showing the restored apse of the small Byzantine church. On the left, the roof of the 14th-century Great Hall.

132. General view from the east, clearly illustrating the excellent natural protection enjoyed by the nor-thern flank and the steep cliffs which separate the outer fortress from the castle proper. On the right, the lower fortress and, above it, Prince John's Tower with the corner-tower of the upper fortress just beyond.

KYRENIA   Page 87

133. Eastern flank of the fortress, with the large Venetian south-east rondel on the left and the Frankish semi-circular tower on the right. The protruding flank of the large polygonal south-west bastion can be seen at the end of the landward-facing fosse on the left.

134. Looking down from the battery platform of the north-west rondel at the forecourt between the old Frankish outer wall and the outlying 16th-century curtain, which has a walled way for cannon. The old gatehouse survived, with the result that a small open forecourt came into being between it and the new gate in the Venetian curtain.

135. The small Byzantine chapel inside the Venetian west curtain. Hemmed in by the stonework of the cur-tain and the large north-west rondel, the little church (known in Frankish times as St George-du-Donjon) dates from the mid-Byzantine period. The dome was restored at a later stage.

136. The northern flank of the fortress – the only one which still displays uninterrupted stretches of masonry dating from the Frankish period. At the far end, the semicircular north-east tower (cf. Photograph 133). Gun emplacements were built into the ground floor in Venetian times.

BELLAPAIS   Page 88

137. The west face of the church, with small belfry, seen through the northern cloisters.
138. Main portal of the refectory, which provides a clue to the lost architectural treasures of the Residence at Nicosia. The rich ornamentation corresponds to decorative techniques commonly employed in the Holy Land, of which only fragmentary examples have survived.

  The marble lintel bears the arms of the Lusignan family (left), the Kingdom of Jerusalem (centre), and the Kingdom of Cyprus (right).

FAMAGUSTA   Page 88

139. The Cathedral of St Nicholas, photographed from the arcades of the former royal palace. The church was built between 1308 and 1315, out of the proceeds of a collection organized by Bishop Guy d'Ibelin in the years 1298–1308. It resembles Rheims Cathedral in many details. The upper parts of the building, notably the towers, were badly damaged by bombardment in 1570–1.
140. Main gate of the citadel, surmounted, like the gates of almost all Venetian fortresses, by the Lion of St Mark. Beneath it is Niccolo Foscarini's inscription, dated 1492. Situated on the south side of the semi-rectangular citadel and guarded by a strong rondel, the gate leads *en chicane* into the inner courtyard of the 14th-century sea-fort, which the Venetians left almost unaltered. The closing scenes of Shakespeare's *Othello* are set in this castle.
141. The large ground-floor chamber on the northern or seaward side of the old sea-fort, built *c.* 1300–10. Relics of an earlier building are embedded in the floor. The windows facing the sea (right) were blocked up by the curtain-wall which was erected during the Venetian period.
142. View of the sea-gate bastion. On the left, the Greek cathedral of St George, probably built towards the end of the 13th century, just before the Latin cathedral of St Nicholas and, like the latter, badly damaged in 1571. Right of centre, the east face of the Latin cathedral. The sea-wall in the foreground dates from the Venetian period and displays the features typical of the early Italian style of fortification, namely, an escarped face culminating in a torus at battlement height.

KOLOSSI   Page 90

143. General view from the south-east, with the sugar refinery in the foreground. The latter may be older than the donjon and shows distinct traces of the Turkish restoration work carried out in 1591.
144. Large fireplace with simple ornamentation in relief, situated in the so-called Commander's living-quarters on the upper floor of the donjon.

BUFFAVENTO   Page 91

145. Southern aspect of the ruins. The rubble-work of the three simple rectangular buildings which constituted the upper fortress has largely disintegrated, but the lower-lying and equally crude buildings of the lower fortress are better preserved and can be clearly seen on the mountain-side. Prominent among them is the massive retaining wall of the gatehouse.

BODRUM   Page 91

146. Castle and town from the north-east, photographed from the modern approach road. On the small rocky mound to the right of the citadel stand the ruins of a block-fort erected during the Turkish period. The long moles enclosing the inner harbour were built in modern times.
147. Engraved slab in the outer west wall beside the castle's main gate. Above, supported by the Virgin and St Peter, the arms of the Order and Grand Master Jean-Baptiste Orsini (1467–76), and below them the date of the curtain (1472) and the arms of the Captain of the castle, F. de Boxols.
148. The oldest tower in the inner fortress, the Tower of France, erected between 1415 and 1420 and bearing the arms of the Pope, France, Grand Master P. de Naillac (1396–1421) and Dragonetto Clavelli. The tower corresponds in type to the more or less contemporary Naillac Tower in Rhodes. On the right, the face of the old citadel; in the background, left, the Tower of England.
149. General view from the east, looking across the large harbour, which is no longer in use. Being naturally protected by steep slopes, this flank of the castle was only guarded by a straightforward curtain which was strengthened at the beginning of the 16th century. An outer skin between 6 and 9 feet thick was added later, almost engulfing the old east corner-tower. Clearly discernible, if only because of the different material used in their construction, are the junction of the bastioned north face and the polygonal Gatineau Bastion.
150. The Tower of England from the north-west. Situated at the southern corner of the outer enceinte and

dating from the first half of the 15th century, it is richly adorned with classical trophies and armorial bearings, and was probably used as an assembly-hall.

151. View of the innner wall, taken from the main gate, showing the south or seaward face. Built in the years 1461–75 and altered so as to permit the mounting of ordnance at the beginning of the 16th century, the south face was severely damaged by naval bombardment in 1915 and the lower battery entirely destroyed. In the background, the Tower of England.

152. View of the castle from across the small inner harbour, which was improved in very recent times and is still used today. This aspect is dominated by the strong north face and its three massive artillery bastions, which almost dwarf the low-lying harbour battery and the west ravelin. Occupying the highest point on the peninsula are the Towers of France and Italy.

153. Carved slab depicting St George, originally mounted on the Tower of Italy but later installed in the forecourt. Beneath the saint are the arms of the Order and of Grand Master Jean de Lastic (1437 to 54), also of Captain Angelo Muscettola (c. 1436 to 7), builder of the Tower of Italy.

RHODES   Page 93

154. View of the town and the Grand Master's Palace, taken from the tower of the small outwork known as Fort San Nicola. In the foreground is the small outer harbour (Mandraki). The Grand Master's Palace was almost completely restored after the Italians occupied the island in 1912. The building had been so badly damaged by bombardment in 1522, earthquakes in 1851 and 1860, and an accidental explosion in 1856, that parts of the ground floor and isolated sections of first-floor wall were all that remained standing. Apart from the substructure, most of which survived, the bulk of the palace in its present form is modern.

155. View of the square in front of the Grand Hospital of the Knights of St John, showing the Hospital itself (left), the Auberge d'Auvergne (in the background, with arched entrance), and the church of Ste Marie du Château.

Founded in 1437 by Grand Master A. Fluviano (1421–37), the Hospital was started in 1440, according to an extant inscription on the building itself. It was finally completed, after work had been interrupted by the Turkish siege, in about 1490. The Auberge d'Auvergne is inscribed with the date 1507 and the name of Grand Prior Guy de Blanchefort. Ste Marie du Château, known during the Turkish

occupation as Kanturi Djami, was probably converted from an earlier Byzantine church in the 15th century.

156. Looking eastwards along the main street of the Castrum. About half-way down on the left stands the Auberge de France, begun in 1492 and probably completed in 1503 by Grand Master Emery d'Amboise. The building was extensively restored in 1913. At the end of the street can be seen the side façade of the Hospital.

157. Small gateway on the west of the town. As had been customary in all Frankish towns in the Holy Land with the exception of Acre, the original fortifications of the residential quarter or Burgus were considerably weaker than those of the Castrum. From the mid-15th century onwards the outer defences were strengthened and no more work was done on the inner fortifications of the Castrum.

158. Frontage of the outwork of San Nicola. The round-tower in the interior was erected by Grand Master P. R. Zacosta (1461–7). The outer platform and its escarped wall date from 1464, but the outermost enceinte was probably added later by Grand Master Pierre d'Aubusson, after the siege of 1480 and the great earthquake of 1481. This outwork was a focus of attack during the siege of 1480, though the Turks failed to capture it.

159. The gate built by Grand Master Emery d'Amboise, with the Grand Master's Palace in the background. Guarded by two small rondels and designed *en chicane*, this gate was started in 1512 as a contribution to the strengthening of the western flank. Armorial plaques attribute the remaining walls of this outwork to the years 1514–22.

160. Strasbourg Master, c. 1290. Louis IX of France (St Louis) 1215-1270 with his consort Marguerite of Provence (d. 1295).
This oak carving is an authentic portrait of St Louis with the beard he had allowed to grow at the beginning of the 1248 crusade. On his breast is a Crusader's cross ornamented with a fleur-de-lys design, and in the crook of his right arm is a model of the Holy Sepulchre of Jerusalem. There is a niche for relics in the back of his head.
The Queen, who clings to the King's arm, carries a lily in her hand (a symbol of the French Royal House). Her head, executed from life, is individual in treatment. In the Middle Ages the smile on a woman's face symbolized feminine perfection.
Jean de Joinville, author of *Histoire de Saint Louis* who had taken part in the Crusade of 1248-1254 with the King and the Queen, donated the group to the Chapel of St Lawrence of Château Joinville as an altarpiece in memory of the Crusade. Private Collection, Berlin.

MAP SHOWING THE SITES OF THE CASTLES

GENERAL BIBLIOGRAPHY

INDEX OF PRINCIPAL CASTLES

THE CRUSADERS' ARENA
(Castle sites are indicated by solid black circles)

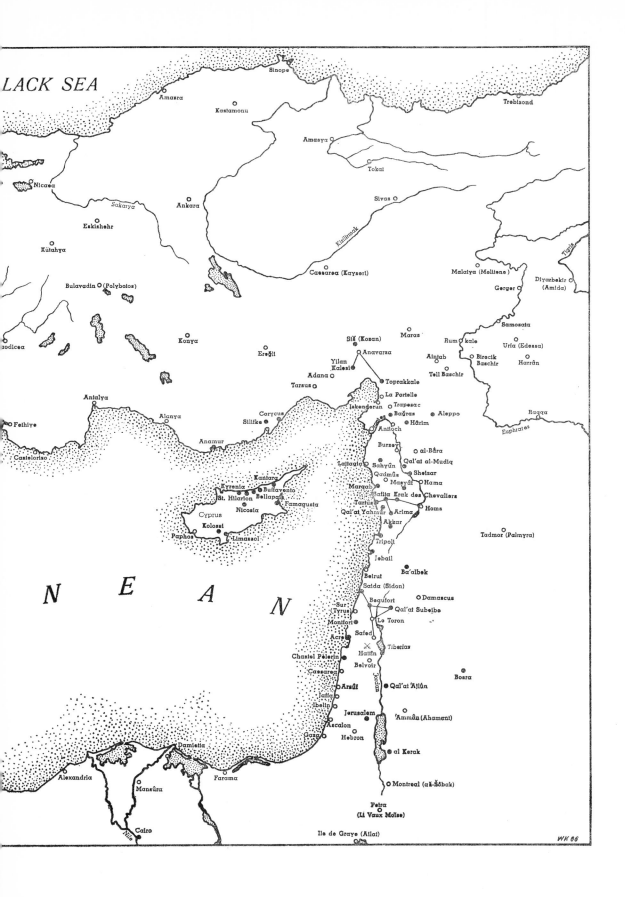

BLACK SEA

Sinope

Amasra

Kastamonu

Trebisond

Amasya

Tokai

Nicaea

Ankara

Sakarya

Sivas

Eskishehr

Kizilirmak

Kütahya

Tigris

Caesarea (Kayseri)

Malatya (Melitene)

Diyarbekir (Amida)

Bulavadin (Polybotos)

Gerger

Samosata

Konya

Sis (Kozan)

Maras

Rum kale

Urfa (Edessa)

odicea

Ereğli

Anavarza

Aintab

Birecik Baschir

Harrân

Yilan Kalesi

Tell Baschir

Antalya

Adana

Toprakkale

Tarsus

La Portelle

Euphrates

Alanya

Corycus

Iskenderun

Trapesac

Aleppo

Raqqa

Fethiye

Silifke

Bağras

Hârim

Anamur

Antioch

Castelorizo

Bursey

al-Bâra

Kyrenia

Kantara

Lattaqie

Qal'at al-Mudiq

Buffavento

Sahyûn

Shelzar

St. Hilarion

Bellapais

Qadmûs

Masyâf

Hama

Nicosia

Famagusta

Marqab

Safita Krak des Chevaliers

Cyprus

Tartûs

Homs

Kolossi

Qal'at Yahmûr

Arima

Paphos

Limasol

Akkar

Tadmor (Palmyra)

N   E   A

Tripoli

N

Jebail

Ba'albek

Beirut

Saida (Sidon)

Damascus

Beaufort

Sur (Tyrus)

Qal'at Subeibe

Montfort

Le Toron

Acre

Safed

Tiberias

Chastel Pèlerin

Hattin

Belvoir

Caesarea

Bosra

Arsûf

Qal'at 'Ajlûn

Jaffa

Jordan

Ibelin

Jerusalem

'Ammân (Ahament)

Ascalon

Gaza

Hebron

al Kerak

Damietta

Alexandria

Montreal (al-Šôbak)

Farama

Mansûra

Petra (Li Vaux Moïse)

Nile

Cairo

Ile de Graye (Ailai)

WK 66

GENERAL BIBLIOGRAPHY

In view of the comprehensive bibliographies and lists of sources given in almost all major works on this subject, reference is made only to the most important supplementary books. With a few notable exceptions, magazine articles have been omitted and no further enumeration of available sources has been made. For a single comprehensive bibliography, see Hans Eberhard Mayer's *Bibliographie zur Geschichte der Kreuzzüge*, Hanover 1960.

Alishan, L. *Sissouan ou l'Armeno-Cilicie*, Venice 1899.

Andrews, K. *Castles of the Morea*, Princeton 1953.

van Berchem, M. and Fatio, E. *Voyage en Syrie* (Mém. Inst. Franç. Archéol. Orient. du Caire, Vols 37–38), Cairo 1913–15 (here referred to as: v. Berchem – Fatio, *Voyage*).

Bréhier, L. *Le monde Byzantin: (1) Vie et mort de Byzance*, Paris 1947; (2) *Les institutions de l'empire byzantin*, 1948.

Brockelmann, K. *Geschichte der islamischen Völker und Staaten*, 2nd Ed., Berlin 1943.

Byrne, E. H. *Genoese shipping in the 12th and 13th centuries*, Cambridge (Mass.) 1930 (Monogr. Mediev. Acad. of America, 1).

Cahen, Cl. *La Syrie du nord à l'Epoque des Croisades et la Principauté Franque d'Antioche* (Inst. Franç. Damas, Bibl. Orient, I), Paris 1940.

Chalandon, F. *Les Comnènes*, Paris 1912, 2 vols.

Conder, C. R. and Kitchener, H. H. *The Survey of Western Palestine, Memoirs of the topography, orography, hydrography and archaeology: I Galilee*, London 1881, *II Samaria*, London 1882 (here referred to as: Conder – Kitchener, Survey).

Creswell, K. A. C. *Early Muslim Architecture, Umayyads, Early Abbasîds and Tûlûnids*, 2 vols, Oxford 1932–40.

- *The Muslim Architecture of Egypt*, 2 vols, Oxford 1952–9.

Deschamps, P. *Les Châteaux des Croisés en Terre Sainte*, Vol. I: *Le Crac des Chevaliers*, Paris 1934; Vol. II: *La défense du Royaume de Jérusalem*, Paris 1939 (here referred to as: Deschamps, *Châteaux I* and *II*).

Dussaud, R. *Topographie historique de la Syrie antique et mediévale*, Paris 1927 (Bibl. Arch. et Hist. 4).

Ebhardt, B. *Der Wehrbau Europas im Mittelalter. Versuch einer Gesamtdarstellung der europäischen Burgen*, Vol. I, Berlin 1939; Vol. II, 1 and 2, Stollhamm 1958–9.

Ebersolt, J. *Orient et Occident. Recherches sur les influences byzantines et orientales en France pendant les Croisades*, Paris – Brussels 1929.

Enzyklopädie des Islam. *Geographisches, Ethnographisches und Biographisches Wörterbuch der muhammedanischen Völker*, 1st Ed., Leyden – Leipzig 1913–34 (here referred to as: *Enc. Isl.*).

Enzyklopädie des Islam. New Edition, Vol. I, Paris–Leyden 1960 (here referred to as: *Enc. Isl. [2]*).

Enlart, C. *L'Art Gothique et la Renaissance en Chypre*, 2 vols, Paris 1899 (here referred to as: Enlart, *Art Gothique*).

- *Les Monuments des Croisés dans le Royaume de Jérusalem. Architecture réligieuse et civile* (2 vols each of text and plates), Paris 1926–7 (B. A. H. 7–8), here abbreviated to: Enlart, *Monuments*.

Fedden, R. *Crusader Castles. A brief study in the military architecture of the Crusades*, London 1950.

Fedden, R. and Thomson, J. *Crusader Castles*, London 1957 (here referred to as: Fedden – Thomson).

Gerland, E. *Geschichte der Frankenherrschaft in Griechenland*, Vol. I: *Geschichte des Lateinischen Kaiserreichs von Konstantinopel*; Vol. II: *Geschichte der Kaiser Balduin I und Heinrich*, Bad Homburg 1905.

Gerola, G. 'I monumenti medioevali delle 13 Sporadi' in: *Annuario Scuola Atene 2*, 1915, 1 et seq.

Grousset, R. *Historie des Croisades et du Royaume de Jérusalem*, 3 vols, Paris 1934–6 (here referred to as: Grousset).

- *L'Empire du Levant. Histoire de la question d'Orient*, Paris 1949.

Hammer – Purgstall, J. von *Geschichte des Osmanischen Reiches*, 10 vols, Pest 1827–35.

- *Histoire de l'Ordre des Assassins*, Paris 1833.

Heyd, W. *Histoire du commerce du Levant* (2nd Ed.), 2 vols, Leipzig 1936.

Hopf, K. *Chroniques gréco-romanes inédites ou peu connues*, Berlin 1873.

- 'Geschichte Griechenlands vom Beginn des Mittelalters bis auf unsere Zeit', in Ersch-Gruber, *Allg. Enzyklopaedie*, Vols 85–6, Leipzig 1867–8.

Jeffery, G. *Description of the historic Monuments of Cyprus*, Nicosia 1918.

Johns, C. N. *Palestine of the Crusades* (3rd Ed.), Jerusalem 1946.

Jorga, N. *Brève histoire de la Petite Arménie*, Paris 1930.

La Monte, J. L. *Feudal monarchy in the Latin Kingdom of Jerusalem (1100-1291)*, 1932 (Monogr. Medieval Acad. of America, 4).

Laurent, J. C. M. *Peregrinatores medii aevi quattuor*, Leipzig 1864.

Lawrence, T. E. *Crusader Castles*, 2 vols, London 1936.

Longnon, J. *Les Français d'Outre-Mer au Moyen-Age*, Paris 1929.

Miller, W. *The Latins in the Levant. A History of Frankish Greece 1204–1566*, London 1908.

Oman, C. W. C. *A History of the Art of War in the Middle Ages* (2nd Ed.), 2 vols, London 1924.

Ostrogorsky, G. *History of the Byzantine State*, Oxford 1956.

Prutz, H. *Kulturgeschichte der Kreuzzüge*, Berlin 1883.

Ramsay, W. M. *Historical Geography of Asia Minor* (R. Geograph. Soc., Suppl. Papers No. 4), London 1890.

Rey, E. G. *Essai sur la domination française en Syrie durant le moyen-âge*, Paris 1866.

– *Etude sur les monuments de l'architecture militaire des Croisés en Syrie et dans l'Ile de Chypre*, Paris 1871 (here referred to as Rey, *Arch. Militaire*).

– *Les colonies franques de Syrie au 12e et 13e siècles*, Paris 1883.

Richard, J. *Le Comté de Tripoli sous la dynastie Toulousaine (1102–1187)*, Paris 1945 (B. A. H. 39).

– *Chypre sous les Lusignan. Documents chypriotes des archives du Vatican (XIVe et XVe siècles)*, Paris 1962 (B. A. H. 73).

Röhricht, R. *Geschichte des Königreichs Jerusalem (1100–1291)*, Innsbruck 1898.

– *Regesta Regni Hierosolymitani*, Innsbruck 1898. *Additamentum*, Innsbruck 1904.

– 'Studien zur mittelalterlichen Geographie und Topographie Syriens', in: *Ztschr. Dtsch. Palästina-Verein 10/1887*, 195 et seq.; *11/1888*, 139 et seq.

– 'Karten und Pläne zur Palästinakunde vom 7. bis 16. Jahrh.', in: *ZDPV 14/1891, 8–11, 87–92, 137–141; 15/1892, 34 et seq.; 18/1895, 173 et seq.*

Runciman, Sir Steven, *A history of the Crusades*, 3 vols, London 1951–4.

Schlumberger, G. *Numismatique de l'Orient Latin. Monographies sur les princes chrétiens de Syrie et de Grèce*, 2 vols, Paris 1878–82.

– *L'Epopée Byzantine*, 3 vols, Paris 1896–1903.

– *Byzance et les Croisades. Pages mediévales*, Paris 1927.

Setton, K. M. (ed.) *History of the Crusades*, Philadelphia, I 1955, II 1962 (in progress).

Sevgen, N. *Anadolu kaleleri, I cilt.*, Ankara 1959.

Smail, R. C. *Crusading warfare*, London 1956.

Spuler, B. *Geschichte der islamischen Länder. I: Die Chalifenzeit. Entstehung und Zerfall des islamischen Weltreichs*, Leyden 1952 (Handb. d. Orientalistik, Vol. 6).

Tobler, T. *Itinera Hierosolymitana et descriptiones Terrae Sanctae bellis sacris anteriora*, 2 vols, 1879–85.

Toy, S. *A history of fortification*, London 1955.

Tuulse, A. *Burgen des Abendlandes*, Vienna – Munich 1958.

Viollet-Le-Duc, E. *Dictionnaire raisonné de l'architecture française du 11e au 16e siècle*, Paris 1867–70.

Waas, A. *Geschichte der Kreuzzüge*, 2 vols, Freiburg 1956.

Wiet, G. 'L'Egypte musulmane de la conquête arabe à la conquête ottomane', in: *Précis de l'histoire d'Egypte II*, Cairo 1932, 109–331.

Youngs G. R. 'Three Cicilian Castles', in *Anatolische Studien 15*, 1965.

INDEX OF PRINCIPAL CASTLES

Colour reproductions are indicated by page numbers in bold type. Italic figures refer to the black and white plates.

Acre, 10, 19, 24, 26, 27, 29, 34, 72-74, **99**, *100*
Acrocorinthus, 33
Akkar, 28, 50, *32*
Anamur, *117*
Antakya, *4*
Arsûf, 11, 22, 28
Aleppo, 10, 12, 16, 19, 66, 67, 90, 91
Arima, 14, 18, 53, *42, 43*

Ba'albek, 18, 54, 55, *44-46*
Bağras, 20, 32, 48, 49, *28-31*
Beaufort, 24, 28, 62, 63, *84*
Beirut, 11, 27
Bellapais, 88, *137, 138*
Belval, *1*
Belvoir, 12, 18
Bethgibelin, 12, 15
Bodonitsa, 82, *118*
Bodrum (Halicarnassus), 37, 91, 92, *146-153*
Bosra, 67, 68, *92-94*
Buffavento, 36, 91, *145*

Caesarea (Kayseri), 9, 24, 26, 28, 31, 74, *101-103*
Calamata, 33
Castel Tornese (Chlemutzi), 33, 34, 82, 83, *119, 120*
Chastel-Blanc (Safita), 1, 14, 18, 22, 28, 51, 52
Chastel Pèlerin, 23, 71, 72, *98*
Chlemutzi, *see* Castel Tornese
Constantinople, 9, 23, 32 ff., 38, *95*
Corycus, 79, 80, *111-114*

Damietta, 23, 24
Dieudamour, *see* St Hilarion

Famagusta, 36, 88-90, *139-142*

Giblet, *see* Jebail
Gabala, 20

Halicarnassus, *see* Bodrum
Hârim, 16, 65, 88, *89*
Hattîn, 19, 20, 22
St Hilarion (Dieudamour), 36, 86, 87, *129-132*

Istanbul, *2*
Izmir, *see* Smyrna
Iznik, *3*

Jebail (Giblet), 20, 22, 26, 27, 64, 65, *85-87*
Jerusalem, 7. 11, **13**, 20, 23, 24, 39, *5-8*

Kantara, 36, 85, 86, *126-128*
Karytaina, 33, 85, *125*
Kayseri, *see* Caesarea
al-Kerak, 12, 20, 47, 48, *23-27*
Kolossi, 36, 90, 91, *143, 144*
Krak des Chevaliers, 18, 22, 25, 27, 28, 38, 39, 59-62, *66-83*
Kyrenia, 36, 87, 88, *133-136*

Lattaqia (La Liche), 12, 20, 27

Margat, 14, 18, 22, 27, 28, 38; *see also* Marqab
Marqab (Margat), 2, 56, 57, 58, *52-61*
Maina, 33
Masyaf, 68, 69, *95*
Mistra, 33, 34, 35, 84, 85, *123, 124*
Mons Peregrinus, *see* Tripoli
Montfort, 24, 28, 74, 75, *104, 105*

Nauplia, 33
Navarino, 33, 83, 84, *121, 122*
Nicaea, 9, 33

Paneas, 16
Pylos, *see* Navarino

Qal'at 'Ajlun, 18, 58, 59, *62-65*
Qal'at 'Marqab, *see* Marqab
Qal'at el-Mudiq, 56, 50, *51*
Qal'at Subeibe, 45, 46, *22*
Qal'at Yahmur, 14, 52, *40, 41*

Rhodes, 34, 36, 38, 93, 94, *154-159*

Safed, 24, 28
Safita, 14, 18, 22, 28, 51, 52, *36-39*
Sahyûn, 10, 14, 17, 18, 20, 44, 45, *12-21*
Saidâ, 11, 20, 23, 24, 26, 27, 69, 70, 71, *96, 97*
Sheizar, 21, 55, 56, *47-49*
Silifke, 80, 81, *115, 116*
Sis (Kozan), 32, 77, *109*
Smyrna (Izmir), 37

Tartus, 50, 51, *33-35*
Toprakkale, 75-77, *106-108*
Tortosa, 18, 20, 22, 26
Tripoli, 12, 20, 22, 23, 26, 28, 42, *9-11*

Yilan Kalesi, 32, 77-79, *110*

Acknowledgements: We wish to thank the Institut Français d'Archéologie Beirut for placing the following aerial photographs at our disposal: 12, 22, 36, 47, 50, 52, 66, 84, 88, 90, 92. The Deutsche Archaeologische Institut Istanbul supplied numbers 2 and 3. Plate 160 was supplied by Professor Metz of the Stiftung Preussischer Kulturbesitz.
All other photographs were specially taken for this volume by A. F. Kersting, London.

THE PLATES

1. BELVAL

2. ISTANBUL

3. IZNIK

4. ANTAKYA

5. JERUSALEM

6. JERUSALEM

7. JERUSALEM

8. JERUSALEM

9. TRIPOLI

10. TRIPOLI

11. TRIPOLI

12. SAHYUN

13. SAHYUN

14. SAHYUN

15. SAHYUN

16. SAHYUN

17. SAHYUN

18. SAHYUN

19. SAHYUN

20. SAHYUN

21. SAHYUN

22. QAL'AT SUBEIBE

23. AL-KERAK

24. AL-KERAK

25. AL-KERAK

26. AL-KERAK

27. AL-KERAK

28. BAĞRAS

29. BAĞRAS

30. BAĞRAS

31. BAĞRAS

32. AKKAR

33. TARTUS

34. TARTUS

35. TARTUS

36. SAFITA

37. SAFITA

38. SAFITA

39. SAFITA

40. QAL'AT YAHMUR

41. QAL'AT YAHMUR

42. ARIMA

43. ARIMA

44. BA'ALBEK

45. BA'ALBEK

46. BA'ALBEK

47. SHEIZAR

48. SHEIZAR

49. SHEIZAR

50. QAL'AT EL-MUDIQ

51. QAL'AT EL-MUDIQ

52. MARQAB

53. MARQAB

54. MARQAB

55. MARQAB

56. MARQAB

57. MARQAB

58. MARQAB

59. MARQAB

60. MARQAB

61. MARQAB

62. QAL'AT ADJLUN

63. QAL'AT ADJLUN

64. QAL'AT ADJLUN

65. QAL'AT ADJLUN

66. KRAK DES CHEVALIERS

67. KRAK DES CHEVALIERS

68. KRAK DES CHEVALIERS

69. KRAK DES CHEVALIERS

70. KRAK DES CHEVALIERS

71. KRAK DES CHEVALIERS

72. KRAK DES CHEVALIERS

73. KRAK DES CHEVALIERS

74. KRAK DES CHEVALIERS

75. KRAK DES CHEVALIERS

76. KRAK DES CHEVALIERS

77. KRAK DES CHEVALIERS

78. KRAK DES CHEVALIERS

79. KRAK DES CHEVALIERS

80. KRAK DES CHEVALIERS

81. KRAK DES CHEVALIERS

82. KRAK DES CHEVALIERS

83. KRAK DES CHEVALIERS

84. BEAUFORT

85. DJEBAIL

86. DJEBAIL

87. DJEBAIL

88. HARIM

89. HARIM

90. ALEPPO

91. ALEPPO

92. BOSRA

93. BOSRA

94. BOSRA

95. MASYAF

96. SAÏDA-SIDON

97. SAÏDA-SIDON

98. CHASTEL PELERIN

99. AKKON-ACRE

100. AKKON-ACRE

101. CAESAREA

102. CAESAREA

103. CAESAREA

104. MONTFORT

105. MONTFORT

106. TOPRAKKALE

107. TOPRAKKALE

108. TOPRAKKALE

109. SIS (KOZAN)

111. CORYKUS

112. CORYKUS

113. CORYKUS

114. CORYKUS

115. SILIFKE

116. SILIFKE

117. ANAMUR

118. BODONITSA

119. CASTEL TORNESE

120. CASTEL TORNESE

121. NAVARINO

122. NAVARINO

123. MISTRA

124. MISTRA

125. KARYTAINA

126. KANTARA

127. KANTARA

128. KANTARA

129. ST. HILARION

130. ST. HILARION

131. ST. HILARION

132. ST. HILARION

133. KYRENIA

134. KYRENIA

135. KYRENIA

136. KYRENIA

137. BELLAPAIS

138. BELLAPAIS

139. FAMAGUSTA

140. FAMAGUSTA

141. FAMAGUSTA

142. FAMAGUSTA

143. KOLOSSI

144. KOLOSSI

145. BUFFAVENTO

146. BODRUM

147. BODRUM

148. BODRUM

149. BODRUM

150. BODRUM

151. BODRUM

152. BODRUM

153. BODRUM

154. RHODES

155. RHODES

156. RHODES

157. RHODES

158. RHODES

159. RHODES

160. ST. LOUIS